Producing

FilmCraft

Producing

Geoffrey Macnab
& Sharon Swart

Focal Press
Taylor & Francis Group
NEW YORK AND LONDON

First published in the USA 2013 by Focal Press
Focal Press is an imprint of the Taylor & Francis Group,
an informa business
70 Blanchard Road, Suite 402, Burlington, MA 01803, USA

Copyright © 2013 The Ilex Press Ltd.
All rights reserved.

This book was conceived, designed, and produced by
Ilex Press Limited, 210 High Street, Lewes, BN7 2NS, UK

Publisher: Alastair Campbell
Associate Publisher: Adam Juniper
Managing Editor: Natalia Price-Cabrera
Editor: Tara Gallagher
Specialist Editor: Frank Gallaugher
Creative Director: James Hollywell
Senior Designer: Ginny Zeal
Design: Grade Design
Picture Manager: Katie Greenwood
Color Origination: Ivy Press Reprographics

No part of this book may be reprinted or reproduced or utilized in any form or by any electronic, mechanical, or other means, now known or hereafter invented, including photocopying and recording, or in any information storage or retrieval system, without permission in writing from the publishers.

Notices:
Knowledge and best practice in this field are constantly changing. As new research and experience broaden our understanding, changes in research methods, professional practices, or medical treatment may become necessary.

Practitioners and researchers must always rely on their own experience and knowledge in evaluating and using any information, methods, compounds, or experiments described herein. In using such information or methods they should be mindful of their own safety and the safety of others, including parties for whom they have a professional responsibility.

Product or corporate names may be trademarks or registered trademarks, and are used only for identification and explanation without intent to infringe.

Library of Congress Cataloging in Publication Data:
A catalog record for this book is available from the Library of Congress.

ISBN: 978-0-240-82374-4 (pbk)
ISBN: 978-0-240-82388-1 (ebk)

Typeset in Rockwell Light

TABLE OF CONTENTS

Introduction 8

Peter Aalbæk Jensen 12
DENMARK

Tim Bevan 22
UK

Jan Chapman 32
AUSTRALIA

Legacy

Michael Balcon 46
UK

Lorenzo di Bonaventura 48
USA

Ted Hope 60
USA

Marin Karmitz 72
FRANCE

Legacy

David O. Selznick 82
USA

Legacy

Dino De Laurentiis 114
ITALY

Jon Landau 116
USA

Andrew Macdonald 126
UK

Edward R. Pressman 138
USA

Legacy

Erich Pommer 150
GERMANY

Lauren Shuler Donner 152
USA

Jeremy Thomas 162
UK

Ron Yerxa & Albert Berger 174
USA

Introduction

A producer's role isn't easy to define. It's a multifaceted job that requires the wearing of many hats, and can vary dramatically depending on the film, and where and how it is being made. Over the years, perhaps one of the few things that has been clear is that those who carry the full credit of "producer" are the only ones eligible to receive the Academy Award for Best Picture. But even that's been challenged recently. The old caricatures of cigar-chomping magnates of the Darryl F. Zanuck variety persist in the public imagination. As do the myths of the original über-producers: the penniless immigrants from Eastern Europe who eventually made it big in Hollywood, such as Adolph Zukor and Samuel Goldwyn. Watch Michel Hazanavicius' Hollywood-set silent movie **The Artist** (2011) and you'll see the familiar archetype of the producer reinvoked in the shape of the calculating Al Zimmer (John Goodman), who decides that silent star George Valentin is past his sell-by date and that the public wants "fresh meat."

The control freakery and creative interference of MGM's "boy wonder" Irving Thalberg is part of movie lore. Thalberg had a hand in everything, though he famously never took a screen credit as "producer." Working firmly within the studio system in its heyday, Thalberg may seem a long way removed from the producers interviewed for this book. Nonetheless, his qualities—taste, tenacity, and vision—remain as important in the film world now as they were in Culver City in the 1930s.

One part mountebank, one part magician, the producer is the ringmaster who keeps the circus going, reconciling the creative and financial demands of his collaborators. Producing requires audacity, as well as shrewd money minding. Oscar-winning British producer Jeremy Thomas (**The Last Emperor**, 1987) says a producer is someone who is able to "flash the cash." A producer is a confidence man or woman. They are selling an idea. It's the producer's faith that convinces the creative team they're actually capable of making the movie and the backers that it can be brought in on time and budget. A producer must have a Napoleon-like flair for logistics, an eye for talent *and* the balance sheet. They must have enough charm to woo investors, combined with the flintiness to strike tough deals—while also having a keen instinct for marketing. However, the context in which producers work can vary enormously, impacting their scope of autonomy and responsibility to different degrees.

For the last few decades in Hollywood, many of the biggest producers have had "studio deals," generally supplying office space on the studio lot, development funds, and production financing. Though these types of producer deals have been scaled back radically in recent years, a producer on the level of Jerry Bruckheimer (housed for many years under the Disney umbrella) hasn't been required to cobble together the money to finance his films for quite some time. Meanwhile, the American independents, who work chiefly outside of the studio system, must have detailed knowledge of things such as bank loans, completion bonds, tax incentives, and the international sales market.

In Europe and throughout most of the rest of the world, film producers operate very similarly to the American independents. They're responsible for gathering their own financing, but also have more flexibility in the types of material and collaborators to work with. One European producer interviewed for this book gives a fabulous example of the stark difference between independent and studio worlds. Andrew Macdonald, the producer of British hits **Shallow Grave** (1994) and **Trainspotting** (1996), recalls his first experience of making a US studio film with a sense of bewildered irony. When he saw the contracts, Macdonald was startled by how much power the "producer" seemed to have. It was only after more careful perusal that he realized the "producer" referred to in the legal documents wasn't him at all. The studio was the producer. He was just an employee, albeit one with a "producer" credit.

On the other hand, in the world of independent production, where films rely on small armies of financiers, the various producer credits can multiply at an alarming rate. There are executive producers, co-producers, associate producers, and assistant producers working alongside the "producer." On one recent European co-production that screened at the Venice Film Festival, a well-known director joked to the press that he hadn't even met many of the producers listed on his film. Some had come on board to enable the production to take advantage of various European soft-money schemes.

On Oscar night, the question of who produced the Best Picture can take on an added urgency. For example, when Paul Haggis' **Crash** was in the Oscar limelight in 2004, a ferocious battle broke out between the financiers and producers over who should have been credited. Lawsuits were flung around between the contesting parties and the controversy reverberated for years afterward. The dispute underlined just how elastic the concept of "producer" had become.

In the French system, where the cult of the auteur still ensures that directors retain the pivotal place in the filmmaking process, producers are generally seen as functionaries. They're not the ones with the vision: they're the handmaidens to the directors. For example, the name Georges de Beauregard doesn't loom large in film history. He produced many of the key films of the French New Wave—**Breathless** (1960) and **Contempt** (1963) among them—but posterity hardly acknowledges that fact. Yet the names of his directors—Jean-Luc Godard, Claude Chabrol, Eric Rohmer, Agnès Varda, and Jacques Rivette—are vaunted and widely known.

In complete contrast, the British film industry always has always been driven by producers. From Ealing Studios' boss Michael Balcon, to **Chariots of Fire** (1981) Oscar-winner David Puttnam, and Working Title Films' luminaries Tim Bevan and Eric Fellner, the names of the producers have often eclipsed those of the directors. Their distinct imprint has been felt on the work too. The plaque left behind when Balcon quit Ealing in the mid-1950s stated: "Here, during a quarter of a century, many films were made projecting Britain and the British character." Puttnam's films tended to be humanistic epics: large-scale movies shot abroad, such as **The Killing Fields** (1984) and **The Mission** (1986). And Bevan and Fellner worked on both sides of the pond, churning out edgy indies, as well as popular British film series, including the **Bean** and **Bridget Jones's Diary** movies.

The producers interviewed for this book come from varied backgrounds. Hong Kong producer Bill Kong (**Crouching Tiger, Hidden Dragon**, 2000) moved sideways into production after years in exhibition and distribution. Los Angeles-based Lauren Shuler Donner (**You've Got Mail**, 1998; **X-Men**, 2000) started out as a camera operator in television. Jeremy Thomas was an editor. Danish maverick Peter Aalbæk Jensen (**Europa**, 1991; **Breaking the Waves**, 1996) was a former rock music roadie and promoter who wanted a quieter life. Andrew Macdonald was an aspiring director who realized while shooting a short film that he was doing everything a producer is supposed to do: securing the budget, finding the locations, hiring the talent. Although some of the interviewees have passed through film school, most make the point that their skills can't be learned in an academic context. They're not like directors, editors or cinematographers, who have specific creative and technical crafts to master. In fact, producer Jon Landau (**Titanic**, 1997; **Avatar**, 2009) says he's still learning on every film.

These producers invariably have extraordinarily close relationships with the directors with whom they work. Whether it's Landau with James Cameron, Aalbæk Jensen with Lars von Trier, or Macdonald with Danny Boyle, the producers act as partners. Another trait they share is a strong sense of optimism. They believe fervently in the vision of the filmmaker and never doubt, in spite of all the obstacles in their way, that the movie they're working on will be completed and will triumph. Some have their magic recipes for making films. Finance them through pre-sales and you can have your budget covered before you start: That was Thomas' formula when he was making epics such as **The Last Emperor** and **The Sheltering Sky** (1990). A formula which doesn't work as easily today. Aalbæk Jensen is a master at co-producing and accessing finance from regional funds and tax shelters. What the producers tell their investors the film will cost and what they tell the foreign distributors isn't always the same number. And both parties know it.

A flair for showmanship is another quality many possess. They use the major film festivals to put their movies in the international shop window. Some may not have access to studio-level marketing budgets, but they know how to get their projects to stand out. If these movies →

are in competition in Cannes or Venice, they're able—at least for a few days—to compete on equal terms for press attention and red carpet hoopla with the Hollywood majors.

Some of the producers interviewed here come from filmmaking dynasties. Kong's father formed Edko, Hong Kong's leading independent exhibition chain. Thomas is the son of British director Ralph Thomas and grew up around the film business. He remembers being given a wind-up Bolex when he was 13 and making home movies. Landau's parents, Ely and Edie Landau, were producers (**The Iceman Cometh**, 1973; **Hopscotch**, 1980). Macdonald is the grandson of writer Emeric Pressburger (**The Red Shoes**, 1948; **49th Parallel**, 1941) and nephew of businessman James Lee, who ran British company Goldcrest.

What also unites these producers is their absolute cinephilia. They're passionate about movies. As Macdonald enthuses, "If someone wants to be a producer, I always say, 'Watch as many films as you can.' If you don't know your stuff, forget it."

These producers have had to adapt to the circumstances of the era in which they've worked. There have been various sea changes in the film business over the last half-century. One of the biggest came in the 1970s, when producers and financiers such as Dino De Laurentiis pioneered the financing of films through the discounting of distribution contracts. Combined with the rise of the video market, this opened the way for independent companies such as Hemdale, Carolco, and Cannon to prosper. It also saw the emergence of a flamboyant new generation of producers—figures like Cannon boss Menahem Golan (famous for signing contracts on napkins with filmmakers from Godard to Sylvester Stallone) and Hemdale's John Daly, the son of a London dockworker who went on to back such movies as Cameron's **The Terminator** (1984), and Oliver Stone's **Salvador** (1986) and **Platoon** (1986).

At the same time, a new kind of US independent cinema was emerging led by filmmakers including Spike Lee, Jim Jarmusch, and the Coen brothers. Unlike their European counterparts, these American filmmakers couldn't rely on soft money or state subsidies. Their producers were therefore obliged to make sure that the films—however idiosyncratic and visionary they often were—recouped their budgets. There was evidence that European and American producers were beginning to work in very different ways. As New York indie champ Christine Vachon once put it, "I have met several filmmakers who've had largely subsidized careers who don't think that an audience is important. In American filmmaking, audience is the be-all and end-all, you could argue too much so, but if there is not a continual dialogue between filmmakers and their audience, the work becomes a little flaccid."

Of course, the idea that European producers were somehow shielded from harsh commercial reality is exaggerated. Danish producer Aalbæk Jensen notes in his interview with typical gallows humor that the first feature he produced, **Perfect World** (1990), sold 69 tickets in Denmark and was a complete and utter commercial flop. Although he had received some state subsidy, he also had sunk his own money into the movie, and the result was that he was driven into bankruptcy with personal debts of about $350,000 that took him many years to pay off. Thomas considers the negatives to the films he has produced as "the family jewels." He still owns them. However, many other producers have had to sign away rights to their films simply in order to get them made.

European producers of the last few decades were also inspired by their American counterparts. That "can-do" spirit epitomized by films like Lee's **She's Gotta Have It** (1986), Todd Haynes' **Safe** (1995, produced by Vachon), Steven Soderbergh's **Sex, Lies, and Videotape** (1989), and the Coen brothers' **Blood Simple** (1984) was emulated across the Atlantic by movies such as Mathieu Kassovitz's **La Haine** (1995), Boyle's **Trainspotting**, and Tom Tykwer's **Run Lola Run** (1998). European production and sales outfits like X-Filme, Wild Bunch, and Figment Films showed much of the same swagger as the trailblazing US indies.

Lines became increasingly blurred as US studios set up their own specialty arms in the 1990s, and relative fortunes were paid at the Sundance Film Festival for distribution rights to indie films. In 1993, game-changing independent distributor Miramax, run by brothers Bob and

Harvey Weinstein, eventually sold to Disney. And European producers began to work ever more closely with the studios. For Europeans, the economic logic is as daunting as it has ever been. They know they will not be able to recoup the budgets of their films in their domestic markets alone. That's why they need to co-produce and make sure their films are distributed abroad. "The great thing about studios is that they are distributors—the best distributors in the world," Macdonald notes, explaining why European producers are often so eager to throw in their lot with US majors, regardless of the loss of control and ownership that may ensue.

Working Title Films, the pre-eminent production company in the UK, used to be owned by PolyGram Filmed Entertainment (PFE), a European would-be studio that hoped to build a distribution network to match that of the US studios. When PFE was sold to Universal in the late 1990s, Working Title Films ended up as part of a Hollywood Studio. This was the Faustian pact Working Title Film's owners Bevan and Fellner struck: the sacrifice of independence in return for reach within the international marketplace.

Producing is an all-consuming profession. Inevitably, sometimes there's a push back between directors and their producers. The creatives want to take charge and resent fiercely the executives pulling the purse strings. "Here am I in this fucking desert, in this fucking sandstorm, making this fucking film, whilst you are fucking your dolly birds on the fucking Riviera," David Lean is alleged to have complained to Sam Spiegel when the producer had the temerity to question just how long Lean was taking to finish **Lawrence of Arabia** (1962). (Lean's words were overheard by the editor Anne Coates, who told the story of his outburst to author Adrian Turner, when he was writing his 1994 book, *The Making of David Lean's Lawrence of Arabia*.) Spiegel had sent his director a telegram stating, "Never has so little been shot in so much time so badly."

Periodically, directors and actors will try to throw off the shackles of their producers. The same instinct that prompted Charlie Chaplin, D.W. Griffith, Mary Pickford, and Douglas Fairbanks to set up United Artists has inspired many other generations of filmmakers who've sought to go it alone. These ventures rarely work in the way that the artists might imagine.

At the same time, producers have often sought to reinvent themselves as directors. They too struggle. The fictional example of Kirk Douglas as the ruthless producer in Vincente Minnelli's **The Bad and the Beautiful** (1952) is a case in point. As a producer, he controls every aspect of the films he works on. His relationship with the filmmakers he hires is virtually that of a ventriloquist with his dummy. He knows everything about the business and craft of film. Yet when he tries to direct a movie himself, he makes a complete hash of it.

What remains clear is that the role of the producer will never be easy to categorize. It constantly changes in relation to the circumstances in which a movie is being made. What is clear, though, is that the best producers remain at the center of the process, from a film's inception to its release, keeping all the plates spinning.

With plate spinning in mind, we would like to express our thanks to the book's editors Mike Goodridge and Natalia Price-Cabrera for their patience and encouragement. We are grateful to Melanie Goodfellow, Alice Fyffe, and Jeff Thurber for their assistance. And finally, we wholeheartedly thank the wonderful producers interviewed in this book for their time, candor, and generous spirit.

Geoffrey Macnab and Sharon Swart

Peter Aalbæk Jensen

"I think I am good at getting the right people aboard. That is more or less the only skill that I have. I face that I can do nothing myself, but at least I can bring the right people together. Who are the right people? That would be producers, financiers, scriptwriters, sometimes actors. Putting the crew and the talent together—that is my talent."

Europa (1991)

Denmark's Peter Aalbæk Jensen (born in 1956) is a true maverick: a former rock music roadie who moved sideways into film, hooked up with Lars von Trier when both men were at a low ebb in their careers, and has gone on to produce or executive produce more than 70 films. Aalbæk Jensen has based his career around a close working relationship with one or two directors. Alongside his long partnership with Von Trier, he has known [Danish director] Susanne Bier since film school days and partly credits her for persuading him to become a producer.

Aalbæk Jensen is a born iconoclast. He is the outsider, the man from the provinces who gatecrashed the cozy Copenhagen media world. It was striking that when he and Von Trier set up Zentropa in 1992, they based themselves at Filmbyen, a former army barracks outside Copenhagen. At the same time, Aalbæk Jensen is a skilled dealmaker who has come up with a financing model that has enabled Von Trier to carry on making films on an ambitious scale. Whether it's working with regional funds, tapping the Council of Europe fund Eurimages, securing advances from loyal tribes of distributors, or setting up offshoots of Zentropa in countries with soft-money schemes, Aalbæk Jensen is an expert at funding movies out of Europe. Bluntly spoken, but often very witty, he has a showman's instinct too.

Europa (1991)— Aalbæk Jensen and Von Trier's first film together—was a critical success and they have gone onto work on such films as **The Kingdom** (1994), **Breaking the Waves** (1996), **Dancer in the Dark** (2000), **Dogville** (2003), **Antichrist** (2009), and **Melancholia** (2011). At Zentropa, Aalbæk Jensen has been involved in everything from Dogme low-budget films to Puzzy Power—hardcore porn movies with a feminist slant—and lavish costume dramas like **A Royal Affair** (2012). He describes his most important skill as being able to choose his collaborators wisely and to sniff out talent. Aalbæk Jensen has also worked with Fridrik Thor Fridriksson, Nicolas Winding Refn, Thomas Vinterberg, and Lone Scherfig. He is currently in production on Von Trier's latest film, **Nymphomaniac**, which stars Charlotte Gainsbourg, Shia LaBeouf, and Stellan Skarsgård.

INTERVIEW

Peter Aalbæk Jensen

"I was quite happy about the rock-and-roll business. It was, of course, extremely entertaining and also extremely tough. I thought, okay, if everybody says the film business can be a rough business, then you should be a roadie!

Gradually, I went more into the organization, working as a stage manager on Scandinavian rock-and-roll festivals. As a spare-time project, I started to make music videos in Denmark. That was before MTV. This meant that the moment MTV entered the scene in Scandinavia, everybody was asking for music videos. We were just about the only ones with some kind of knowledge of making them. I had my own production company together with two of my friends, but it was just for fun—something to do in my spare time when I was not working with music.

Then, I entered the Danish Film School as a sound technician student in 1983. I was thinking that I didn't have the brains for producing (a lot of people will still agree). I thought producing was about using the money cleverly—although not in a criminal sense. That inspired me, but I didn't think I was competent enough for that.

I studied with [Danish director] Susanne Bier. She thought it was a disaster that I was studying to be a sound technician. She could see that I was not that interested in it. She persuaded me to move over to production. I switched over [courses] after two years. The last two years were in production. I was producing Susanne Bier's student films. Of course, making films for no money was complicated, but Susanne was a great partner for me because she was also at that time quite obnoxious and didn't have any respect for anything. However, we are still working together 28 years later. She is an extremely loyal person. I learned a lot from her.

Lars von Trier had left the Film School by then and so I didn't know him at all.

I graduated from Film School in 1987 and went out and produced my first feature film—and I went bankrupt with that. It was called **Perfect World** (1990) and it sold 69 tickets in Denmark. It was just a total flop—an extreme art-house movie. We financed it with some money from the Danish Film Institute and I invested some money in it also. It took me 12 years to repay the debt. Was it a good film? Yes, but I never understood what the story was about. It was so arty farty you couldn't understand the movie. That was maybe why it sold only 69 tickets. The director was Tom Elling, who was cinematographer on Von Trier's debut film, **The Element of Crime** (1984).

Since I was bankrupt, I needed to go out and find some work just to pay the bills. I worked then as a production manager on commercials. On a commercial, I met Lars. At the time you could say that, career-wise, he was bankrupt in Denmark. He was so hated here. That was for good reasons because he was really an asshole. He was so hated that nobody wanted to work with him. Since I was bankrupt also, I think we felt we were two flops who could unite.

I owed something like $350,000. We pay very high taxes in this country and with the remaining money, I had to feed my family and repay my debts. Those were tough times.

Lars had tried to produce his second film **Epidemic** (1987) himself. He had also learned that maybe he wasn't that good at producing.

01 The Element of Crime (1984). Michael Elphick (left), Me Me Lai (center), and director Von Trier (right)

"We wanted to make a sect in a way also—to make Zentropa a place where you more or less are for a lifetime. That was important for me, for Lars, and for Susanne. That was the feeling…we were not making a film together—we were making a career together."

Choosing the right team

(02–03) Aalbæk Jensen takes a very pragmatic approach toward producing. When it comes to working with directors or hiring crew and collaborators, the trick (he suggests) is to pick people you trust and can rely on. Susanne Bier **(03)** and Lars von Trier **(02, left)** have been permanent fixtures throughout his career.

"I think I am good at getting the right people aboard. That is more or less the only skill that I have. I face that I can do nothing myself, but at least I can bring the right people together. Who are these right people? That would be producers, financiers, scriptwriters, sometimes actors. Putting the crew and the talent together—that is my talent. When you're not good at something, you have to compensate with something else. I think I have developed some good antennae for social interaction. I think I can feel when a talented person is sitting in front of me. I never want to see the CV of a person I employ. I don't want to check their background. I think I can feel instantly if they are worth investing in. Without bragging, I must say most of the people I have worked with have become important characters in the local scene here. Maybe that is a little gift I have been given by God."

I think he felt he needed a partner in business. He had spent a lot of time on projects that were not produced. He was quite frustrated and I was bankrupt. Then we did a commercial for a French transportation company. Afterwards, Lars asked me if I could help him with his third feature, **Europa** (1991). I thought okay, I have only heard bad things about the guy, but do I have any alternatives? No! I just jumped into it. I think he felt the same also. We felt like two drowning characters in the ocean, trying to help each other to survive.

Europa was a big production. That was before the great European co-production adventure. In Denmark, I think we made eight films a year with a lot of public support, but nobody had ever collaborated with any other country other than maybe Sweden or Norway. It was really a risky project, but we were young and didn't know all the problems we faced. In that sense, maybe that was what made the project come through. We didn't know all these hurdles that were involved in pulling the project together. I think I had 27 different financing partners. I didn't have a contract because nobody had made anything like that before. I didn't have a sales company. None of the sales companies wanted to work with us. I couldn't even speak English, so we had to start totally from scratch. It was still thrilling.

The name of our production company Zentropa came from **Europa**. After the film, I thought, okay, that was it. We agreed to make one film together, Lars and I, and that was fine. Since **Europa** was recognized as a kind of larger manifestation of Lars' talent, suddenly there were some bigger UK, German, and French producers who wanted to work with Lars. Even though he is a strange character and not always 100 percent easy to cope with, he is extremely loyal. The fact that I helped him with **Europa** when he was fucked meant that he said to these big German, UK, and French companies, all right, do whatever you want, but we have to include Peter. I don't know that many directors who have said "no →

"A goddam efficient machine"

(01–02) Since venturing into European co-production with **Europa** (1991), Aalbæk Jensen and Zentropa have refined the art of working with many different countries and sources of financing on their films. This has meant sometimes moving away from Denmark. It has also required tact and delicacy when dealing with potential foreign partners.

"You can't just open offices around Europe and start getting money out of your subsidiaries," the producer notes. "You also have to deliver something in return. I think (when we work abroad) we have a sincere interest to work with local talent and to use whatever we have learned to help the local talent. I think that is why we are accepted. We are there to repay previous and coming contributions by the investment from Zentropa in local talent. But when we are making the bigger projects and everybody sticks together, we join forces with five or six Zentropa offices around Europe and we agree this film will be made, then it is a goddam efficient machine."

thanks" to (Constantin Film boss) Bernd Eichinger and that level of producer to be loyal to the local producer. I don't think anybody else would have done that. You could say my career has very much been with Lars and Susanne, two extremely loyal people who for some strange reason have chosen to be loyal to me. I think they would laugh their heads off if I said I had any comments on the script. As you know, I am a guy from the provinces, a redneck from the outskirts of Denmark. I'd say this project stinks or that's a crappy title. That is the kind of dialogue I have with Lars and Susanne. I have no sense at all of what they are doing with the scripts or what you might say is the artistic side of it. I am there to support them and to carry them in the market. They are much more intelligent than I am.

When we started with **Europa**, we had nothing at all. We didn't know anything about anything, but with the next films we were building on the past—and everything is easier if you have built it before. From there, it was just a case of repeating and refining the instruments. When we started Zentropa, Lars, of course, wanted me very much to focus on his own films, but that was too claustrophobic for me. I also had the possibility of working with Susanne Bier and other directors. From there on, we needed to have staff. We needed to have an organization. Both Lars and I have always been keen that the films should be produced in an industrial framework.

When we started becoming a little bit successful, I felt that the success could be a threat also: that suddenly we could see ourselves in the media ghetto of Copenhagen, drinking cappuccinos together with the rest of the media gang. I felt we needed to do something completely different. Then we found this military base—Filmbyen—here on the outskirts of Copenhagen in a concrete suburb with a lot of immigrants and social problems. We said why doesn't the film business move out of the inner fancy circus and then meet reality. I think that, combined with Lars' idea of the Dogme movement, was popular at that time.

We wanted to make a sect in a way also—to make Zentropa a place where you more or less

BREAKING THE WAVES

(03) This film was one of the sensations of the 1996 Cannes Film Festival. Emily Watson (left) won near ecstatic reviews for her performance as Bess, the young Scottish woman who believes that she can communicate with God. Ironically, the film wasn't intended to be shot in Scotland at all. Nor was Watson first choice.

The religion of producing

The Danish producer speaks—only half jokingly—about producing in religious terms. He talks about faith and likens shooting a movie to embarking on a pilgrimage.

"What makes a good producer? It's a question of if you are able to believe…that you have the possibility to believe in people and projects. That's what counts. It's very easy to face all the problems if you have the almost religious feeling that it is something sacred you are traveling with. You can communicate that (to the financiers) if you believe. You can say you are in the light of God if you are a believer."

04 Susanne Bier's Oscar-winning film **In a Better World** (2010)

are for a lifetime. That was important for me, for Lars, and for Susanne. That was the feeling… we were not making a film together—we were making a career together.

We went down the TV route with **The Kingdom** (1994) because we were broke and needed to do something that could make a turnover quickly. We were trying to get **Breaking the Waves** (1996) financed and that was really hard because that was, at the time, quite a big budget. We needed something else to survive. Television seemed good. Both Lars and I, when we were ten years old, had seen a French black-and-white TV series called **Belphegor**, about a masked ghost who wandered round the basement of the Louvre Museum in Paris. That was where the idea came from for taking a big hospital in Copenhagen and putting some ghosts into it. That was the birth of **The Kingdom**. We made it for a fixed price. That gave us liquidity and turnover so we could get **Breaking the Waves** started. We treated this mini-series as if it was a feature film and sold it like that, without re-editing the television series. It was just put together in eight reels, screened in Venice and then sold afterward for theatrical release.

At that time, there was no export of Danish films and not at all of Danish television. We actually retained all the foreign rights to **The Kingdom**, which DR [Denmark Radio] thought had a value of zero. We were quite pissed that we couldn't get any rights for Scandinavia—DR took that—but in the end we got the most valuable part—we got all the foreign rights.

Breaking the Waves cost around $7.5 million. One thing was to finance it. The other thing I faced was to finance the financing…to arrange the banking of all these contracts. That was a →

"When we started with **Europa**, we had nothing at all. We didn't know anything about anything, but with the next films we were building on the past—and everything is easier if you have built it before. From there, it was just a case of repeating and refining the instruments."

THE IDIOTS

(01–02) Lars von Trier's **The Idiots** (1998), along with Thomas Vinterberg's **Festen** (1998), helped usher in the Dogme wave of low-budget films made under the terms of the so-called "Vow of Chastity." Aalbæk Jensen says that he was struck by how accessible the Dogme pictures turned out to be.

"Dogme was Lars' idea. It also became an industry platform. We ended up making 12 or 14 Dogme films along with another Danish company, Nimbus Film. It was extremely fun to make these Dogme films and it was also very interesting to see how they turned out, because we gave a hell of a lot of freedom to the directors. Most of them are quite entertaining, quite funny, and more commercial than we would have expected. Isn't that strange?"

> "You could say my career has very much been with Lars and Susanne, two extremely loyal people who for some strange reason have chosen to be loyal to me."

heavy problem because no Danish banks had ever gone in and financed contracts in the movie business. We had to educate ourselves in working internationally and financing co-productions. We also had to educate our banks on how to operate in the film industry.

Lars has always been very pragmatic. As long as he knows in advance, he understands when he needs work outside of Denmark, and accepts actors from other countries and is prepared to shoot in regions where it is profitable for us to be. There have never been discussions about that. You can see how awkward it can be sometimes with all these point systems there are when you are co-producing in Europe. Some of the best artistic collaborations Lars has had have been with people he has been more or less forced together with for financial reasons. Then, they ended up becoming friends and working together voluntarily.

You can be pragmatic as long as you have a director who is good at always switching the story to match the financing. **Breaking the Waves** should originally have taken place in Holland. We couldn't get any money there so we thought, okay, Scotland, and especially the Outer Hebrides, was interesting in terms of what it could give to the story. I actually think it became a better film than if it had been shot in the Netherlands. Lars always creates a strange universe where it works that there are people of different nationalities.

We had Helena Bonham Carter. We were crazy about having her on **Breaking the Waves**, but then she pulled out. We have always had this philosophy that if someone pulls out we don't try to persuade them to stay. We've always felt we can get someone else who would be better for the film. Emily Watson entered the casting session with bare feet. We were sure when we →

03 Dancer in the Dark (2000), directed by Lars von Trier, and starring Björk and Catherine Deneuve

saw the first casting session that she was our "Bess" (as the character is called in the film). Of course, I follow all the ups and downs in the film. After **Breaking the Waves**, everything we (at Zentropa) had learned with Lars we used with Susanne Bier and Lone Scherfig, and the other great directors of our company. I thought it was quite natural that slowly the projects became bigger and bigger, and then the company slowly became bigger, with more employees. It wasn't an overnight process and I thank God for that.

When Lars started working with American actors and big international stars that was a new game. I wouldn't say that we were always successful in playing that game. But I think maybe we have some advantages coming from a shitty little country in that we could behave in another way and be more frank and direct—and maybe more naughty. That was a totally new game to learn. It was one thing to have all these problems and good times with the talent but—Jesus Christ!—agents and managers. That was something to learn.

To me, it's a privilege to come from a small country. We have no national pride. We don't think of ourselves as superior. That makes it easier for you to deal with other nationalities.

For once, we said with **Melancholia** (2011), we had a great film with no controversy. We agreed that Lars should surprise everybody by being nice and gentle. That was the one and only time in the company history we had a strategy!

01 **Dogville** (2003), directed by Lars von Trier, starring Nicole Kidman

02 Charlotte Gainsbourg in **Antichrist** (2009), also directed by Lars von Trier

"When Lars started working with American actors and big international stars that was a new game. I wouldn't say that we were always successful in playing that game. But I think maybe we have some advantages coming from a shitty little country in that we could behave in another way and be more frank and direct—and maybe more naughty."

[And that strategy imploded when Von Trier infamously said, "I understand Hitler," during a Q&A session for the film's premiere at the Cannes Film Festival in May 2011.] Besides that, the marketing strategy has always been improvised. It has been really fun to have it as a playground to generate stories. From stupid things like running around naked, to saying provocative things, we've always being able to generate a story, big or small.

Every day still feels fresh and inspiring to me. I think I am the most privileged guy in the world, to be able to make films out of Europe.

At the end of the day, producers should fight for the film and the director, and also sometimes fight against the company. Sometimes, the company should fight against the film. It's a better position that you have an executive representing the company and a producer representing the film. That's a better cocktail in my judgment."

03 Melancholia (2011), directed by Lars von Trier and starring Kirsten Dunst

Tim Bevan

"Scripts are what matter. If you get the foundations right and then you get the right ingredients on top, you stand a shot… but if you get those foundations wrong, then you absolutely don't stand a shot. It's very, very rare—almost never—that a good film gets made from a bad screenplay."

Atonement (2007)

In commercial terms, Working Title Films, the production company that Tim Bevan helped found and co-chairs, is the most successful UK outfit of its generation. From **Bridget Jones's Diary** (2001) to **Four Weddings and a Funeral** (1994), **Notting Hill** (1999), and **Love Actually** (2003), from **Nanny McPhee** (2005), and **Bean** (1997) to **Atonement** (2007), and **Shaun of the Dead** (2004), their films have made hundreds of millions of dollars. Working Title Films has also been instrumental in creating British stars (Hugh Grant, Keira Knightley) and in talent-spotting writers and directors (Richard Curtis, Joe Wright). Bevan entered the British film industry via the world of pop promos in the 1980s. Working Title was formed in 1983. The company's breakthrough came when he and Sarah Radclyffe (his original partner in the company) produced **My Beautiful Laundrette** (1985).

When Michael Kuhn set up PolyGram Filmed Entertainment (PFE) in 1991 with the ambition of creating a European-based "studio" with the reach and distribution firepower of a Hollywood major, he looked to invest in Working Title Films. At this point, Radclyffe stepped aside and Bevan's current business partner Eric Fellner came on board. Under Bevan and Fellner, Working Title Films quickly blossomed. Both producers targeted the international market. The success of **Four Weddings and a Funeral** was followed by a string of hits. At the same time, they worked with the Coen brothers on films such as **Fargo** (1996) and **The Big Lebowski** (1998), while also overseeing low-budget British successes such as **Billy Elliot** (2000).

When PFE was closed down in 1999, Working Title came under the ownership of Universal, however, Bevan and his team retain extraordinary autonomy. Universal trusted the company to greenlight their own movies up to a reported budget of $35 million. The Working Title filmography is very varied. Spy thrillers, zombie comedies, period dramas, and kids' movies sit alongside the romantic comedies that have been their biggest successes. In early 2012, when this interview was conducted, Working Title's slate was as full and varied as ever, wrapping up **Anna Karenina**, preparing **Les Misérables**, discussing a new Bridget Jones, and working full throttle on Ron Howard's Formula One racing movie, **Rush**.

INTERVIEW

Tim Bevan

"To be a producer, I think you've got to be a fairly sophisticated jack of a lot of trades and probably king of a few. [Independent UK producer] Duncan Kenworthy once described the art of producing as "herding a lot of cats in the same direction." The same direction is the most important thing. All movies are made up of a group of personalities, usually some pretty big ones. They are made up of a lot of people with different skill bases and different opinions. A good movie always comes about when you manage to get those people working together in a smooth direction.

You have to have a nose for a story and to understand the development process. I guess the next big thing is putting the right group of people together to make the film—picking the right director to match up with the right writer and then with the right line producer, heads of department and right actors. There is a chef like quality to that. A good creative producer will have been there at the beginning of the process. Quite often, it will have been their idea to make the film. It's about keeping that basic vision clear in your head all the way through because there are going to be a million billion things that try to fog that vision. Holding that idea of why **Atonement** (2007) will make a good film and reminding people of that, all through the process, is an important factor.

Early on in my career, I tended to be more interested in the line production side of it—how the money got spent and all the rest of it. What I am much more interested in now is the idea of what makes a movie, what the movie is, developing it into a decent script and then putting the right ingredients together to get it turned into a film and maintaining that creative overview all the way through.

There is very little training you can have to be a good producer. Funnily enough, I do think that a legal training or a financial training is not a bad place to begin. Just on the practical side, there is an awful lot of legal work and numerate work that you just have to understand. I think that ordered thinking that comes from both of those disciplines is a pretty good thing to be able to apply to producing. Not that I had either—I hasten to add! I tumbled into the film business. My background was being a runner at Video Arts. I had the aspiration from the start to produce and I was lucky I got into it early on by producing music videos when music videos were just beginning. I skipped that whole thing of working my way up through the ranks, which I think was a blessing. I don't think that necessarily trains you at all well to be a film producer. Being a production manager is not the same as producing at all.

David Puttnam was an early role model because he was doing rather well when I started out. He is a man who made films he believed in. My favorite film-producing book is *Memo from David O. Selznick*. Basically, it covers all aspects of producing. I've still got it on my desk. He [Selznick] was a genius of a producer. He was over-involved in his productions. He was more into micro-management than I certainly am. But I think the thoroughness of thought was impressive. One of the important things in being a producer is to ensure that everyone's quality control is at a high level. One of the reasons that **Tinker Tailor Soldier Spy** (2011) is so good is that although we had limited resources, we had a very, very clever director [Tomas Alfredson] directing the movie. Tomas inspired all the people who were working in every department to do the very, very best that they could do. They were inspired by him. They went the extra mile. They didn't care about the money. They just wanted to make it good. That is the dream position to be in on a film. If you get the level of every single thing up to a certain point, then the audience appreciates it.

Ultimately, films are a director's medium. They have control. It is my job or Eric's [Fellner] to create the right environment for them to do the best job they can. When a film is being made, the director is in charge. You [as producer] create the box, which is either a financial one or a creative one, and providing they [the directors] stay in there, they do their job. I don't have the

"Ultimately, films are a director's medium. They have control. It is my job or Eric's to create the right environment for them to do the best job."

patience to direct! You have to have that myopic, intense patience to be a good director, and it's just not what my skillset is.

Eric and I had known each other. We were on parallel paths. He had made **Sid and Nancy** (1986). I had made **My Beautiful Laundrette** (1985). The two of us had worked in music videos. We had both assembled films independently. Although we're not that similar in character, our skill base is extremely similar. Michael Kuhn [at PFE] was looking to invest in Working Title and he suggested I should find a partner who I could go on this journey with. Sarah [Radclyffe, Bevan's original partner at Working Title when they co-founded the company in 1983] wanted to make smaller movies. She didn't have the ambition that I did of creating a big filmmaking machine.

I like to make movies at whatever level that →

Picture partners

(02) Bevan and business partner Eric Fellner collaboration has yielded many huge box-office successes. They try not to get in each other's way and make the best business and creative decisions possible for Working Title. They don't stop to talk about or analyze their process, they simply have an obvious rapport. As Bevan puts it, this is a "very stable, mutually respectful relationship where we absolutely think pretty much alike on most of the big issues."

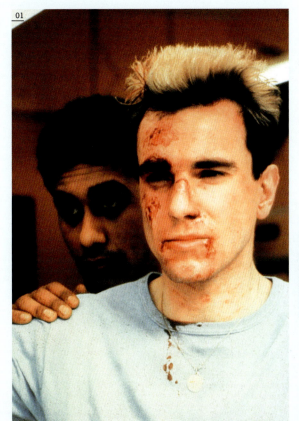

01 **My Beautiful Laundrette** (1985), directed by Stephen Frears. The film was originally made for TV, but after being warmly received at the Edinburgh Film Festival, was given a theatrical release

03 The Coen brothers' **Fargo** (1996)

04 **Shaun of the Dead** (2004), directed by Edgar Wright and starring Nick Frost and Simon Pegg

Sequels and franchises

(01–04) The Working Title attitude toward sequels and franchises is pragmatic, but not cynical. If there is a compelling creative reason to revisit a character (and a strong enough screenplay to stand comparison with the original film), Bevan and his team are open to bringing back characters like Bridget Jones or Nanny McPhee. It helps that there is (as Bevan puts it) a "pre-built" audience for the new films, but he insists the company never makes sequels for the "sake of it." **(01)** Bridget Jones's Diary (2001) was followed by **(04)** Bridget Jones: The Edge of Reason (2004). **(02)** Nanny McPhee (2005) paved the way for the even more entertaining **(03)** Nanny McPhee and the Big Bang (2010).

FOUR WEDDINGS AND A FUNERAL

(05–08) **Four Weddings and a Funeral** (1994) was a key film in Working Title's evolution. Here was a British romantic comedy that was unashamedly commercial and that was marketed and distributed by PolyGram with a zest more commonly associated with Hollywood studio fare. Bevan had had successes before, notably with **My Beautiful Laundrette** (1985), but this was a hit on a different scale. In the British film industry of the 1980s and early 1990s, producers funded by broadcasters and public bodies didn't dare to think that their movies could find huge audiences internationally. **Four Weddings and a Funeral**, which made a star of Hugh Grant **(07–08)**, was instrumental in changing that way of thinking.

> "You need to learn from your failures and from your successes. I always say enjoy the process and learn from the process because the result is going to be pretty fast whichever way it goes."

people go and see. I always felt then that the British film industry was a little under-ambitious. You need resources basically. You need to make films for a slightly bigger budget. They don't need to be gigantic. There's a way you can put more production value, bigger names, bigger stories together.

PolyGram was looking to diversify from music into visual media. We—Michael Kuhn and I—had known each other from music video days. The proposition when he bought properly into the film company was that PolyGram would start a distribution and financing arm. These film labels would just be film production entities. Really, that is what Working Title is today. What we set up in 1992 is pretty much what we have 20 years later.

The break-up of PolyGram [sold by Philips to Seagram in 1998 and merged into Universal Pictures] was disappointing at the time. But, also, you can't hang around. You've got to get on. There are peaks and troughs in this business and you've just got to learn to live with both of them.

Universal [WT's current owners] don't interfere in the films we make. They don't have to make the films we present to them, but they don't tell us what to produce. For the last 20 years we have worked out of either Oxford Street or Marylebone Street. This is a core group of people who are all British. Some of our filmmaking friends are American, some are English, and some are Swedish. The basic company is a British company. We are culturally British and there is a Britishness to pretty much everything that we do.

We were very anxious about it [being owned by Universal] because we thought they would squash us, but we were very lucky. When we first started working with Universal, there was a woman called Stacey Snider running the studio. She was a fantastic collaborator. She had brilliant taste. She saw what we could bring as an additional string to her bow. She didn't expect us to make "Money 3." She wanted us to make the quality movies and felt they existed well with her slate. We got going and made a few pictures that did quite well—so that is the way they treat

PRIDE & PREJUDICE

(01) **Pride & Prejudice** (2005) was considered a risky prospect when Working Title first embarked on the project. This wasn't the typical British costume drama. Its director Joe Wright was making his feature debut. The lead actress Keira Knightley, playing Elizabeth Bennet, was already well-known thanks to **Bend It Like Beckham** (2002) and **Pirates of the Caribbean** (2003), but it wasn't at all certain that she'd be able to carry a period piece. Costume dramas are often attacked by critics for playing it safe. In this case, Tim Bevan and his collaborators were taking a risk by venturing into Jane Austen territory with such an untested cast and crew. The film tested incredibly strongly and reached a younger audience than would normally be drawn to such fare. Its success paved the way for Working Title to collaborate with Wright and Knightley again on another literary project, the adaptation of Ian McEwan's *Atonement*. Both films may have been taken from books but they had what Bevan calls an "edge" about them.

NOTTING HILL

(02–03) In 1999, after the controversial closure of PolyGram Filmed Entertainment, Working Title became part of Universal. Here was Britain's most successful production company owned by a Hollywood major. Bevan and his business partner, Eric Fellner, were originally nervous about a Hollywood major owning the UK's most successful production company, but they had leverage in the deal because Universal was keen to get its hands on the completed rom-com, **Notting Hill**. Their lawyer, Skip Brittenham, helped negotiate them a deal that would give them an extraordinary level of autonomy over the films they would go on to make.

us now. They don't expect us to wander in with the next **Battleship** (2012), but they do expect us to wander in with a film that they can be proud of and that is going to be made at a relatively good and sensible budget, which will relate to the size of audience that it might find.

We are open to people we find interesting and who are good at what they do. I was introduced to Richard Curtis by his agent when he was trying to set up **The Tall Guy** (1989). He had a script. **The Tall Guy** happened to be Richard's first movie. We got going on that and have worked with him ever since. Edgar Wright, Paul Greengrass, and all these other creative relationships have always started with a script or a project idea.

Scripts are what matter. If you get the foundations right and then you get the right ingredients on top, you stand a shot…but if you get those foundations wrong, then you absolutely don't stand a shot. It's very, very rare—almost never—that a good film gets made from a bad screenplay. We spend time with writers. We work on the script. One of the important things we do at Working Title is that when we know we are →

04 **Bean** (1997), starring Rowan Atkinson

TINKER TAILOR SOLDIER SPY

(01–02) Bevan says that one of the key challenges of producing is ensuring that all the key creative personnel are "inspired" and "ready to go the extra mile." That, he believes, was the case on Tomas Alfredson's **Tinker Tailor Soldier Spy** (2011), a John le Carré adaptation that belied its relatively modest budget.

going to make a film, we mentally start the development process again in our heads. For too many people, the endgame is the fact that you're going to make the movie. We think that is the beginning of the race rather than the end of the race. Luckily, we're in a place where we've had more success than failure in our career. Our word goes a little bit further than most and our passion will go a little bit further than most. Many of the best films that I have been involved in on paper didn't look like a starter. But when you add the right passion and the right creative ingredients to it, then they become a viable movie.

Eric and I had made several movies each and were ten years into our careers before **Four Weddings and a Funeral** (1994) came along. We took it in our stride. Ultimately, we are an industry—and in any industry, if you make people money, life gets easier. I guess we learned that big time from **Four Weddings and a Funeral**. It freed us to do things we may not have been able to do otherwise. It hit a moment in time. Once in a while—and it is only once in a while—those low-budget films will come through and do the business. They hit the zeitgeist.

Was it a source of pride making a film as complex and as ambitious as Paul Greengrass' **Green Zone** (2010)? I think you regret the amount of money we spent on it, but you learn from each outing. You need to learn from your failures and from your successes. I always say enjoy the process and learn from the process because the result is going to be pretty fast whichever way it goes. I am proud of **Green Zone**. Would either Paul or I set out to make that same film again? No way! We learned it was a bit out of control, that it cost too much money, and that the equation wasn't a viable one...whereas

03 **Green Zone** (2010), a Bevan and Paul Greengrass collaboration starring Matt Damon

> "One of the important things in being a producer is to ensure that everyone's quality control is at a high level. One of the reasons that **Tinker Tailor Soldier Spy** (2011) is so good is that we had a very, very clever director [Tomas Alfredson] directing the movie."

when we went out on the preceding film, **United 93** (2006), we got it exactly right. We had exactly the right price for a film on a tricky subject that then found an audience. Did we set out to make **Green Zone** on the size that it ended up? Of course not, but you get caught up in the journey, and you've got to stick with it.

Sometimes you pursue things that should be dead. You do pursue films that would be better off not made. That comes from hubris a little bit and also you just spend so many hours, days, and weeks on something that you can't be objective enough to think this should never get done. Sometimes, you just lose sight of things.

With the **Bridget Joneses** and **Nanny McPhees**, I don't see any point in returning to them unless there is some sort of creative reason for it. Of course, if there is a pre-built audience for the film because it is the second one rather than the first one, that helps get it made. But we would never do it for the sake of it because, now, we don't have to! The truth of it is that in Britain there aren't that many movie stars and there aren't that many places to make decent-sized pictures. When you get on with people and you have success together and all the rest of it, why not give it another run?

With Eric, occasionally things will not go the way you want them to, but on the whole it is a very stable, mutually respectful relationship where we absolutely think pretty much alike on most of the big issues. We don't actually tend to do films together on the whole. He is somebody you 100 percent trust. It is one of those things where we know that one plus one is adding up to more than two. We have the same desire to pursue quality wherever possible and to try to stay on our toes and respond to what is going on in the world.

The British film industry has always punched a little bit above its weight. It always tosses up people who can make commercial films like on the Bond movies, the Harry Potter movies, and the Ridley Scotts and the Paul Greengrasses who'll basically make their money and livelihood through Hollywood. There's a local industry that is made up of smaller films and unique voices, which is primarily public money and television backed. Sometimes, interesting people and films emerge from that. One thing that's happened since I started, and which Working Title is at the forefront of, is that there is a very big local audience that will come out for these movies when we get them right. That's very different from when I started. Be it a romantic comedy, a Rowan Atkinson film, a Richard Curtis film or a good-quality film like **Tinker Tailor Soldier Spy**, if you get it right, they come out in big numbers.

A typical Working Title film would be driven by its script. It would be driven by character and by a decent story. It would be unlikely to be driven by visual effects. What's a prototypical Working Title film? Probably **Pride & Prejudice** (2005)—it had a great story, decent script, and we put a little spin on it by putting an unknown director [Joe Wright] and at that point a very young actress [Keira Knightley] into the mix too. There was a bit of risk, a bit of edge to the process as well.

04 **Atonement** (2007), adapted from Ian McEwan's novel by the same name and directed by Joe Wright

Jan Chapman

"I would say **The Piano** was one of the pivotal experiences of my life, but I went on to have a wonderful experience producing **Lantana** with director Ray Lawrence, which was a completely different film. You recreate little worlds, little lifetimes, with a new set of people. That's one of the great things about producing—the creation of a set of relationships and a project at the end of it. It is entirely satisfying!"

Bright Star (2009)

Jan Chapman is part of a generation of Australian filmmakers and producers who emerged in the wake of what became known as the Australian New Wave of the 1970s. At Sydney University (where she studied English literature), she was part of the Sydney Filmmakers Co-Op. She met the filmmakers Gillian Armstrong and Phillip Noyce (later her husband), and gained practical experience of exhibition and distribution, as well as directing her own short films.

Chapman subsequently spent over a decade at ABC TV, directing and producing. During this period, she first encountered Jane Campion, whose TV drama **Two Friends** (1987)—scripted by Helen Garner—she produced. Her first feature film as producer was **The Last Days of Chez Nous** (1992), directed by Gillian Armstrong and also scripted by Garner. By then, she and Campion were already planning **The Piano** (1993), which was eight years in gestation. Although she didn't produce Campion's debut feature **Sweetie** (1989), or her films **An Angel at My Table** (1990) and **The Portrait of a Lady** (1996), she was a script consultant on the last two films.

After **The Piano** won the Palme d'Or in Cannes, Chapman was given a development deal with Miramax. However, she preferred to nurture her own projects in Australia. Through Campion, she was put in touch with Shirley Barrett, whose Camera d'Or-winning **Love Serenade** (1996) she produced. With Campion, she went on to produce **Holy Smoke** (1999) and **Bright Star** (2009). Her other credits include Barrett's **Walk the Talk** (2000) and Ray Lawrence's **Lantana** (2001). She has also served as an executive producer on films by talented young Australian directors, among them Cate Shortland's **Somersault** (2004), Paul Goldman's **Suburban Mayhem** (2006), and Leon Ford's **Griff The Invisible** (2010). She is currently in the early stages of development on a new feature with Campion called **Runaway**, based on an Alice Munro short story.

INTERVIEW

Jan Chapman

" I think a good producer can identify somebody who has a vision that is strong enough to be worth making a film from—so that means a director or a writer, maybe a book. It's really the ability to find the subject or the person who can bring it to fruition best. For me there are certain projects that I am instinctively attracted to—I suppose generally ones that show something insightful about the human condition. A new or original way of understanding people is what really attracts me. I remember in particular seeing Jane Campion's short films and the humorous way they pinpointed the absurdity of the way we all behave toward each other. That immediately attracted me. I sat up in my seat with amazement that somebody could identify these strange physical or verbal habits of people, which really tell you so much.

I started making films at Sydney University as a director. I then worked in the drama department of the ABC (Australian Broadcasting Corporation) as a director and then as a producer. I began in educational television. That was very interesting because you would have to produce films as well as direct them. They were films about everything—science, a fairy story, all kinds of subject matter. That was really a very useful discipline and they had quite low budgets as you can imagine.

I would have seen Jane's films in my early days there and I did have the opportunity to offer her an actual job. That was pleasing for her because she said nobody else had offered one. She made one film in particular called **Two Friends** (1986) written by Helen Garner, who is quite a well-known Australian novelist. I was working on the script with Helen and I thought she was a terribly insightful person about the way people behave. I really thought Jane was the right director, but I was afraid she would not love it as much as I did. She has an original vision and I wondered if I could put the two of them together. But it was a perfect match. They really understood the ability the other had to make something fresher and stronger.

I was really passionate about the study of English literature and I do feel that is a good base on which to know how to tell a story. I would say that my concept of how to make a drama is based on Shakespeare, and on many poets and novelists that I have adored. In fact, often when I read books about screenwriting now, I have a lot more trouble coming at the science of filmmaking through those contemporary theory books. I guess I would always go back to the study of English literature. That is what is in my bones and I guess they were lessons that were very fiercely ingrained in me from a long time ago. I was the kind of child who spent a lot of time daydreaming on my own. I wrote a book in primary school that wasn't a particularly great one, but that [passion for literature] was always there. My father worked in finance. I grew up in Sydney. My mother was a home duties mother, but she had a big interest in art and literature as I discovered.

At Sydney University, I met people who were making films, in particular Phillip Noyce—to whom I was married at the end of my university days—and Gillian Armstrong. We were all involved in the Sydney Filmmakers Co-Op, which

01 **The Last Days of Chez Nous** (1992), directed by Gillian Armstrong and starring Kerry Fox. This was the first feature Chapman produced

Inspiration and the Australian New Wave

In the early 1970s, the Australian New Wave galvanized filmmaking in the country. Major new directors like Bruce Beresford, Peter Weir, George Miller, and Gillian Armstrong emerged. Chapman was later to work with Armstrong. She is also fulsome in her praise for Weir, who enjoyed a major international hit with **(02) Picnic at Hanging Rock** (1975).

"There was a financing structure called 10BA in the country whereby a lot of films were made through tax incentives. There were a lot of historical dramas around that period that were very successful too. I remember Peter Weir was a great inspiration because he was so incredibly original and daring in the way he made films, but also psychically interested in people and attitudes. I guess that is what attracted me. His films were shown at the Co-Op. I remember Phillip Noyce was in one of his shorts called **Homesdale** (1971). Weir was and still is a big inspiration."

was a co-op of filmmakers who wanted to find the means of distribution and exhibition themselves. It was a terribly exciting time in terms of the feeling that you really were in control of the whole process. I've always felt making a short film is not very different to making a long one. You've still got to do all the same things: find the story, find the money, find the right people to work on it. At the Co-op Cinema, we would actually see the audiences reacting to the films immediately. You really did have the sense of putting on a show and of creating something for the audience. Also, I think the collaborative nature of that group and making films is something I learned there.

When I was directing short films, Sandra Levy, who now runs the Australian Film, Television and Radio School, was one of my first producers. I also worked as an assistant director, did continuity,

> "For me there are certain projects that I am instinctively attracted to—I suppose generally ones that show something insightful about the human condition. A new or original way of understanding people is what really attracts me."

bits of wardrobe—everything! You really did feel that you contributed no matter what your role was. I guess that's part of the philosophy I have. With the people I work with, I want everyone to be proud of the film, and to feel that they really have contributed to making it.

I think the fact that I know what it feels like to be a director and to want to express your personal vision made me sensitive to directors. Very early on, I met people who I thought had a very obvious, natural gift like Phillip [Noyce] and →

> "I was really passionate about the study of English literature and I do feel that is a good base on which to know how to tell a story. I would say that my concept of how to make a drama is based on Shakespeare, and on many poets and novelists that I have adored."

Jane [Campion]. I think I was an okay director, but I had to work it out whereas they were visually instinctive. Those two people both have much more extrovert personalities than I do. They are showmen. They love to tell a story, they love to be the center of attention. That is not my personal nature. I am more somebody who is willing to support, to sublimate my own ego in order to see something happen that I really believe in.

When I left the ABC, I made two features in two years—and I had my only son. It was kind of a busy period. Jane [Campion] and I had started working on [the script of] **The Piano** (1993). **The Last Days of Chez Nous** (1992) (directed by Gillian Armstrong) was written by Helen Garner who I had already worked with on **Two Friends**. Directors are all individuals. You try to embrace whatever style works for each of them. With **The Last Days of Chez Nous**, I had started developing that with Helen and then I had to talk Gill into coming back from America to work on it. She had a career going there and it was a big decision to come back. It took a little while to convince her to do it. At the time I guess Gill was a lot more experienced as a feature director than I was as a feature producer. We had known each other since the Co-Op days. Then we hadn't been so close for a while. We hadn't seen each other much probably for a decade. I suppose it began as a slightly more formal relationship in a way, slightly more reserved than it became. I was pregnant during that shoot. I was very grateful to her. She was very encouraging saying yes, we could do this film, and I could have a baby, and everything would be fine. I did appreciate that. Gill has a group of people she likes to work with, including the fabulous Mark Turnbull who was associate producer on that [and on **The Piano**] and first assistant. She really did teach me the value of surrounding yourself with experienced people who really know their area.

With someone like Jane Campion, it is obvious that she has a visual style that is extremely strong and instinctive, very clear and comes to her at the same time as an understanding of the story.

01

02

Devoted, Down Under

Chapman takes her identity as an Australian producer very seriously. She has done most of her work in the country. "The Australian industry matters to me a great deal," she says. "I think there is a spirit that is quite specifically Australian. There is a European tradition and an **Easy Rider** (1969) from America tradition—a bold, Scorsese tradition. It felt that because we were so far away, we could embrace the best of both, the more radical of both. I don't know if this theory stands up, but that is the way I have always felt—that this industry can be distinct and that the best work is done when we make work that is true to our culture and the tone of our national character." **(03)** Chapman accepting the Australian Film Institute (AFI) Award for Best Film for **The Piano**. From left to right: Actor Sigrid Thornton, former Prime Minister Paul Keating, and Chapman.

However, she will then refine it and refine it, storyboard it and work it out very carefully. Directing is something that is a natural talent, but that which people who do well continue to refine.

I feel like Jane and I grew up together. We did those films at the ABC together. She showed me an eight-page treatment of **The Piano** years before we finally made it. We imagined how we'd cast it and finance it. I feel very comfortable working with her. With her insights into the way people behave and why a character might choose to do a certain action, she goes very deeply into the psychology of character. She tries to really understand who they might be. She really will push herself further than I've ever seen anyone else do to try and understand what she is dealing with in the story she has made up. You might start out with an outline for a story, but then one has to find the nuances, sub-plots, and turning points. Jane does that by really understanding the characters—how they might have behaved in situations that may not actually end up in the screenplay. Jane and I have always worked together and separately, which has actually been very good for the relationship and the friendship. She has encouraged me to work with other directors.

It was eight years from when Jane first showed me the small initial treatment of **The Piano** until →

01 **Love Serenade** (1996). From left to right: Actor Miranda Otto, director Shirley Barrett, actor George Shevtsov, actor Rebecca Firth, and Jan Chapman

02 **Love Serenade** (1996)

04 Chapman worked as a script consultant on Jane Campion's **The Portrait of a Lady** (1996), starring John Malkovich and Nicole Kidman

THE PIANO

(01–06) Chapman and Campion could have cast only Australians or New Zealanders in **The Piano** (1993). The $6 million budget was entirely covered from a single source, French company CiBy 2000, and the production wasn't under pressure to go after "names." Nonetheless, the director and producer decided to use actors audiences would know. "Of course, Holly [Hunter] and Harvey [Keitel] were not the people who might have been suggested by our American financiers. The great irony of Holly's casting is that the part was written for a very tall woman," Chapman recalls. "It was Holly's insistence in wanting to be seen through her agent at the time that made Jane see her. When we saw her in a screen test, she had all of the power and passionate intensity and stubborn quality that we wanted this woman to possess."

Chapman was startled by the sheer professionalism of Holly Hunter and Harvey Keitel, and New Zealander Sam Neill. "Holly had to do sign language. She hadn't played the piano for many years and so she re-learnt. She took piano lessons. There was so much character preparation for the roles. It was very exciting to be around that kind of commitment." **(05)** Chapman on set with Jane Campion during filming.

"It was eight years from when Jane [Campion] first showed me the small initial treatment of **The Piano** until we finally produced the film. She said, I don't think I am ready to do this. She had an insight into her own need to mature as a filmmaker and as a person."

> "With someone like Jane Campion, it is obvious that she has a visual style that is very strong and very instinctive, very clear and comes to her at the same time as an understanding of the story."

we finally produced the film. She said, I don't think I am ready to do this. She had an insight into her own need to mature as a filmmaker and as a person.

On **The Piano**, I think it was my naïveté that enabled me to deal with this new world I suddenly found myself in. It was quite complex dealing with the [American] agents, but it was just something I treated in a matter-of-fact kind of way. We had a lot of freedom on **The Piano** because it was fully financed by Ciby 2000. At the time, François Bouygues, who ran the company, had the idea to finance a number of directors around the world. It was like a patron situation. For example, David Lynch made a film for Ciby and so did Almodóvar. The person who was really instrumental in that marriage was [critic and programmer] Pierre Rissient. At the time, he was coming to Australia to identify work he thought could be presented at Cannes. He found Jane's short films and her TV film **Two Friends**. We went to Cannes under his guidance really. He came to see us when we were starting to finance **The Piano**. I was trying to do it in quite a conventional way. We went on a long trip through America where we met many, many, many distributors. He said he believed **The Piano** could be financed by this man, Bouygues. Really, I didn't think it would happen.

01 **Lantana** (2001), starring Geoffrey Rush and Barbara Hershey

02 Chapman on the **Lantana** set with director Ray Lawrence

On the pitfalls of the US system

What put Chapman off about the studio system in America was the chorus of "different opinions about casting and scripts and so much contradiction in the vision." She decided it worked better for her to be working directly with just a director and/or writer. "I find a lot of different notes from a lot of different people too early can impede the process."

Craft work

From her background in TV and at the Sydney Filmmakers Co-Op, Chapman has knowledge of almost every element of filmmaking. She encourages camaraderie on her film sets and tries to make every technician feel that their contribution is vital.

"I worked as an assistant director, did continuity, bits of wardrobe—everything! You really did feel that you contributed no matter what your role was. I guess that's part of the philosophy I have. The people I work with, I want everyone to be proud of the film and to feel that they really have contributed to making it."

(03–05) On **Holy Smoke** (1999) Chapman worked again with Campion and Harvey Keitel, this time with British actress Kate Winslet. **(04)** Chapman on set.

Janet Patterson, who did the costume design—and also the sets and costumes for **Holy Smoke** (1999) and **Bright Star** (2009)—was at the ABC with me in the early days. She met Jane in those days and designed **Two Friends**. She has been a collaborator all along the line. She is somebody who is interested in costume from a character point of view. She is very intelligent and very interested in the project as a whole. You get the costumes meaning more than just a superficial decoration. They are really intrinsically part of the character. She was very aware of the color palette of the whole film and she had a very deep understanding of character. The cinematographer Stuart Dryburgh came from an art background too. He was very involved in the conceiving of the visual palette as, of course, was the production designer Andrew →

BRIGHT STAR

(01–04) Chapman cites her experience studying English literature as fundamental to the way she approaches producing. Her sense of what makes a drama work is more rooted in her knowledge of literature than in anything she has learned in screenwriting manuals. This knowledge stood her in good stead when she was producing Jane Campion's **Bright Star** (2009), about the English romantic poet John Keats, and starring Abbie Cornish and Ben Whishaw. **(01)** Campion with Chapman at the film's New York premiere.

> "You know people more intimately than you do in normal friendship because you've spent so much time working on subject matter that means you often talk about things that you mightn't do in normal small talk."

McAlpine who, although a resident of the UK, was in fact a New Zealander and very conscious of the special qualities of the landscape and culture.

Jane and I always choose our collaborators very carefully. With [composer] Michael Nyman, although the music he had done for Peter Greenaway wasn't really what we were looking for, we had the idea of having quite a contemporary feel to the classical music. Michael came out very early to Australia during pre-pre-production and talked through the feeling of the music. Actually, he would play us ideas. Often, composers don't find it that easy to play something for you. It certainly helps when you are trying to find a language for the music. Neither Jane nor I were particularly sophisticated in terms of our knowledge of music. He just would demonstrate ideas. We were able to work with him to devise a style of music. Again, he was the perfect collaborator—very amusing and engaging, and exploratory.

Jane went back to Australia before the Palme d'Or was announced. I was left there [in Cannes] on my own. It was a very strange experience. Then there was a personal tragedy in her life. She had this amazing success and this deep, deep personal tragedy. It was a complicated time. I guess the point is that life is part of producing. Knowing the people you're working with, you become part of their whole lives really. You know people more intimately than you do in normal friendship because you've spent so much time working on subject matter that means you often talk about things that you mightn't do in normal →

05 **Somersault** (2004), directed by Cate Shortland, and starring Abbie Cornish and Sam Worthington

> "I think the fact that I know what it feels like to be a director and to want to express your personal vision made me sensitive to directors."

small talk. I do feel like I've had very close relationships with the directors I've worked with.

There was a moment after Cannes where I felt a great deal of loss for the project. It had taken over my whole life for a long time. I would say **The Piano** was one of the pivotal experiences of my life, but I went on to have a wonderful experience producing **Lantana** with director Ray Lawrence, which was a completely different film. You recreate little worlds, little lifetimes, with a new set of people. That's one of the great things about producing—the creation of a set of relationships and a project at the end of it. It is entirely satisfying!

Financing a film is never at all easy, but you find great collaborators. On **Bright Star**, Pathé was very much with us along the road. [Pathé boss] François Ivernel came on board very early when Jane had the idea. Once again, there were quite serious constraints about the budget. People understood what kind of film it was. It was not an obvious box-office hit really. I feel I've had incredible commitment from distributors I've worked with again and again, and who really believe in the work. That makes it possible. There is a great worldwide society of people who love film. When you go to film

01 Suburban Mayhem (2006), directed by Paul Goldman

festivals, you realize what a great thing it is to be part of that group. There's a shared understanding between people.

If an idea takes hold of me, I am so determined to make it that really nothing will get in the way. I can see it on the screen."

02–03 Griff the Invisible (2010), directed by Leon Ford and starring Ryan Kwanten

born in 1896, Michael Balcon was a patrician, headmasterly figure who ran Ealing Studios along very strict lines. "Benevolent paternalism" is the phrase most often used to describe his regime. He could be stubborn and chauvinistic. "He didn't really approve of women behind the camera," producer Betty Box noted. However, in his own mild-mannered way, he was also innovative and even quietly subversive.

Balcon's moment of epiphany came at the end of World War II when he began to steer Ealing Studios toward making intensely British comedies that offered their own barbed critique of post-war British society. Ealing was "the studio for good British films." In **Passport to Pimlico** (1949), **Whisky Galore!** (1949), and **The Titfield Thunderbolt** (1953), small communities banded together against the big, bad bureaucrats. Only in the gleefully amoral **Kind Hearts and Coronets** (1949) did the studio deviate from its values of decency and restraint.

Everything about Ealing under Balcon emphasized the collective against the individual. Ealing movies were full of character actors (most prominently Alec Guinness) rather than stars. Although some very talented directors worked in the Ealing stable (Alexander Mackendrick, Robert Hamer, and Charles Crichton among them), the Ealing movies were made by teams rather than by individual auteurs. They nearly all carried Balcon's imprimatur. On one level, as he acknowledged, the films were deeply formulaic. "We take a character or a group of characters, and let them run against either an untenable situation or an insoluble problem. The audience hopes they will get out of it, and they usually do: the comedy lies in how they do it."

Balcon's own achievement as a producer was to take his own group of characters—the directors, the technicians, the actors at Ealing—and mold them together. As historian Charles Barr has pointed out, Balcon set out in the late 1940s to make films that were both popular and true to British national identity. Almost uniquely among movie producers, he advocated a modest and self-effacing approach. There was an economic

01 Michael Balcon (1948)

02 The Ladykillers (1955)

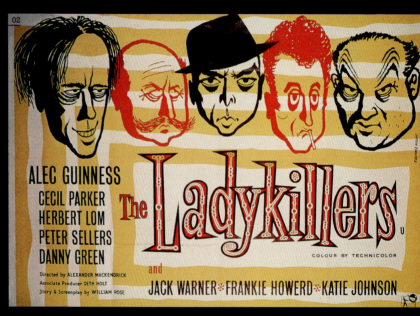

> "We take a character or a group of characters, and let them run against either an untenable situation or an insoluble problem. The audience hopes they will get out of it, and they usually do: the comedy lies in how they do it."

logic to his strategy. If budgets could be capped, then the films stood a chance of recouping their costs in the domestic market alone. As long as they were profitable, Balcon could maintain his control. He could keep his autonomy without interference from the Rank Organisation, which had taken over Ealing in 1944.

Not that Balcon had always pursued this small-scale artisan approach. His career as a producer is far more varied than his time at the helm of Ealing in the late 1940s might suggest. This quintessential English gentleman was the son of Eastern European Jewish immigrants. The Birmingham-born producer began in the film business as a distributor, partnering with Victor Saville in the early 1920s to set up Victory Motion Pictures. Balcon and Saville went on to form Gainsborough Pictures, producing several early Alfred Hitchcock movies as well as some films featuring Ivor Novello—as close as British cinema of that period came to its own matinee idol. In this period, Balcon often appeared to be pursuing a strategy diametrically opposed to the one he embraced at Ealing a generation later. He worked with stars, paying a small fortune to recruit Hollywood actress Betty Compson to star in **Woman to Woman** (1923) and **The White Shadow** (1924). In the 1930s, he tried to nurture home-grown stars too, working with Jessie Matthews and George Formby. During his brief stint heading up MGM's UK operations, he oversaw such glossy, escapist fare as **A Yank at Oxford** (1938).

Throughout his career, whatever style of films he was making, Balcon was always very clear about the primacy of the producer. As he wrote in 1933, "the work of the film producer is to determine the choice of subjects, of directors and of artistes, for every picture, and to decide the cost to be borne...he is the sponsor, and the guide, and the ultimate court of appeal... the kind of energy which the producer must stimulate and direct is based upon the creative and artistic impulses of directors, writers, cameramen and artistes. Such impulses are so personal, but they constantly require the close attention of one directing mind to blend them into the harmonious unity which is essential for any successful achievement in a form of entertainment which depends upon the specialized work of so many different hands." Balcon died in 1977 at the age of 81.

03 Kind Hearts and Coronets (1949), starring Alec Guinness

04 Downhill (1927), starring Ivor Novello

Lorenzo di Bonaventura

"What prepared me more for producing than any single job I've had was running a white-water rafting company with my college roommate for many years. Rafting is about getting a group of people—who are head-strong and don't like to be told what to do—down a destination with supplies, and with great panache."

Transformers: Revenge of the Fallen (2009)

Entrepreneurial and determined, Lorenzo di Bonaventura came to Hollywood after studying intellectual history at Harvard and collecting an MBA from Wharton. The New Hampshire-raised producer held executive positions at two major studios before becoming a full producer in 2003 with a deal at Paramount.

He got his start in a business position at Columbia Pictures and quickly found his way into the power corridors. He transferred to Warner Bros. where he ultimately rose to head of worldwide production. There he oversaw the blockbuster franchises **The Matrix** and **Harry Potter**.

Di Bonaventura credits his "Warners education" for giving him the skillset and mindset that breeds sound moviemaking. He's known for this tenacity and his creativity, as well as for being responsible to the financial side of filmmaking. He's accustomed to the steady flow of studio backing, but he doesn't take it for granted. "You're still convincing someone to spend a lot of money, and no one parts with a lot of money easily," he says. "Every movie feels that way to me."

As a producer, Di Bonaventura cooked up two action franchises for Paramount—**Transformers** (2007, 2009, 2011) and **G.I. Joe** (2009, 2013). Along the way, he also birthed hits such as spy thriller **Salt**, starring Angelina Jolie, and action ensemble **Red** (both released in 2010 through other studios).

He continues to keep his slate packed with still more original projects as well as sequels. "There's no time to rest on your laurels and there's no time to believe you've got something done until it's done," he says.

INTERVIEW

Lorenzo di Bonaventura

"What prepared me more for producing than any single job I've had was running a white-water rafting company with my college roommate for many years. Rafting is about getting a group of people—who are head-strong and don't like to be told what to do—down a destination with supplies, and with great panache. You have to motivate up to 30 people while trying to organize ten days' worth of food, water, medical supplies, etc. Nothing goes exactly as you plan it. The water's too high or the shuttle driver doesn't show up. There are so many variables that are literally like producing. A few forces inevitably led me into the movie business. As a kid, the two things that drove me were movies and sports. I'd watch movies late into the night on television and play sports by day. But the idea of the movie business as a business didn't really register. It didn't occur to me until much later in life that you could actually do it as a job.

After the rafting business, I tried various more serious jobs. I then made the decision to go to business school (at the University of Pennsylvania's Wharton School) because I didn't know what I wanted to do and I realized it would give me two years to figure it out. I thought hard about what would actually motivate me and get me excited, and I concluded it was the movie business. I moved out to Los Angeles and did interviews, and finally got a job at Columbia Pictures. It was a business job, evaluating and selling ancillary market rights to films. I did that for a period of time, but I experienced a rapid shift in the two and a half years I was at Columbia—there were three different studio heads. My big break came from (former Columbia Pictures president) Dawn Steel. I had found a way from ancillary rights into distribution and marketing, primarily distribution. Dawn took me under her wing and I then worked directly for her as a troubleshooter or a man of many hats. Working in the office of the president, I learned a lot about all the different functions of the studio. Then, when she was leaving Columbia, she helped me get a job with [then-production executive] Lucy Fisher at Warner →

01 Transformers: Dark of the Moon (2011), directed by Michael Bay

"The thing about producing is that it takes an amazing amount of stick-to-it-ness, because you're constantly being rejected on so many different levels. When you start out, you're looking at a script or you've got an idea, and you don't know how many times somebody's going to say 'No' to you."

G.I. JOE: THE RISE OF COBRA

(02–04) "With each movie, there is always a new challenge and new things to learn," says Di Bonaventura, who has mounted many effects-laden action franchises, including the **G.I. Joe** films (2009, 2013). "How you keep a character alive in the middle of these giant movies becomes an interesting and increasingly creative puzzle. Visual effects and 3D keep improving. What I like about the job is it's not going to stay in one place ever."

Moviemaking machine

(01–06) Di Bonaventura created two robust branded-entertainment franchises at Paramount, **Transformers** and **G.I. Joe**. The fourth **Transformers** film is planned for 2014, and the second **G.I. Joe** film is due for release in 2013. Both properties came from toymaker Hasbro. "I started my Hasbro relationship with **G.I. Joe** (2009)," says the producer. "It was the first Hasbro property I set up for a movie. Ironically, **Transformers** (2007) became the first to get made. Hasbro had asked what other properties interested me. I mentioned Transformers and they asked why, as I am too old to have grown up with it. I explained that I'd watched brothers and sisters of friends while growing up and seen how effective Transformers was in drawing a certain age group. As a business man, I felt the idea that it had a deep mythology and fan base gives you a shot." Many have told Di Bonaventura that **Transformers** was destined to be a franchise. "I wish that's what every executive had said when we first talked to them about it," he says. The producer remembers that the movie was a difficult sell because people had a hard time imagining how the bulky, awkward circa-1980s robots would translate to film. "I knew the robots were going to be cool," he says. "The visual effects capabilities have transformed—excuse the pun—what is possible and continue to change. I didn't know what else was going to do it, but I was sure about the robots."

It eventually came together when DreamWorks and Paramount had partnered. "DreamWorks had just worked with Michael Bay on a movie and suggested him to me," Di Bonaventura says. "Michael turned this into an amazing franchise. Frankly, the difference between the biggest filmmakers in our business and the next group down are the ones who have actually seen through a franchise. It's a real creative juggling act to get through three and, in our case, now a fourth movie. How do you keep coming up with something new and interesting enough to sustain it that long? It's very easy to lean back on what you just did in the movie before. They stop working unless you keep reinventing and you need to better yourself each time."

(01) Director Michael Bay on set with Shia LaBeouf on **Transformers: Revenge of the Fallen** (2009). **(02)** Di Bonaventura with actor Tyrese Gibson (2009). **(03)** Di Bonaventura with director Michael Bay on the set of **Transformers** (2007).

"The number of robot and alien movies now is gigantic, but it wasn't when we were doing the first **Transformers**. Anytime you try to step outside of what's been working, people look at it and they don't quite know if they should embrace it or not."

"One of the things that disappoints me about the business right now is that the idea has taken hold that a polarizing movie is not commercial. My experience has always been that there will be some people who won't go and see it, but there will be people who will be very fervent about going. And they'll convince other people to go."

Bros., where I made the transition to a full creative position. One of the things that was really daunting at the time—I was 33 years old—was that everyone was telling me I was too old to be a creative executive. People were saying, "How are you going to do that job? It's a young person's job." It was a very bizarre thing to be told, but it probably helped me a great deal because it just made me more terrified and more determined. Five-and-a-half years later, I was president of production and did that for roughly seven years. I had a great experience at Warner Bros. and was lucky to work for [former Warner Bros. chairmen/CEOs] Bob Daly and Terry Semel. They taught me a lot that's been of great value throughout my career.

After Warner Bros., I became a producer at Paramount and I've been a producer now for about nine years. [Former Paramount chairman and president] Jonathan Dolgen and Sherry Lansing were incredibly welcoming to me as I was making the transition, so I had a soft landing. And [Paramount chairman/CEO] Brad Grey has continued to be very supportive. I've been lucky that those regimes I've worked for at Paramount have been so embracing of the kind of movies I like to make and very supportive of me personally. The thing about producing is that it takes an amazing amount of stick-to-it-ness, because you're constantly being rejected on so many different levels. When you start out, you're looking at a script or you've got an idea, and you don't know how many times somebody's going to say "No" to you. In retrospect, people look at **Transformers** (2007) and say it was an obvious franchise. Well, it wasn't obvious when we were trying to sell it, and we were rejected a lot of times. It could have turned out to be the thing that so many people said to us, which was, "That's kind of a goofy idea. A boy and his robot? What's that?" They would look at the 1980s cartoon with

03 **Salt** (2010), starring Angelina Jolie

Believing the unbelievable

The Matrix (1999) "was an amazing challenge. It was about perseverance and the Wachowskis. The filmmakers had to be incredibly persistent because they had to keep rewriting the script. We had to keep trying to make it better. While I was involved, they did 11 drafts of the script before we finally got greenlit, maybe more. They had to take a lot of rejection and hang in there and believe that I, as a studio executive, was not going to give up on them and was going to continue fighting. A lot of mutual belief was going on. God bless Keanu Reeves, because if he'd never said 'Yes,' we would have never gotten that movie made. It was finally greenlit when I was president of production at Warner Bros. Even then, I had a very hard time. It was so out of the realm of what was being made. But as a prudent company, everyone was assessing whether to risk a large amount of capital. So I never thought that their debate was wrong or misguided in any way, it was just that I believed and needed to convince them of the same." Di Bonaventura's belief paid off and two more films followed—**The Matrix Reloaded (01)** and **The Matrix Revolutions (02)**, both 2003.

1980s animation. The robots were these bulky, lumbering things. So it was difficult for people to imagine it was going to be a cool movie. That's true with a lot of big ideas—they have a built-in skepticism that you have to overcome. In part, because usually the really big ideas step away from what everyone's been doing to a certain extent. The number of robot and alien movies now is gigantic, but it wasn't when we were doing the first **Transformers**. Anytime you try to step outside of what's been working, people look at it and they don't quite know if they should embrace it or not.

During my Warners days that was definitely true about **The Matrix** (1999). When we tried to put that movie together, we made very few believers for a very long time. For five and a half years we fought to get that made—and fought is the operative word. Within the studio, it represented something that nobody had really →

> "I bet if you look at most successful movies, there's a story in each one of them about a producer who had to stick to believing in something that very few people were willing to believe along the way."

01 **Three Kings** (1999), starring George Clooney, Mark Wahlberg, and Ice Cube, and directed by David O. Russell

tried. And outside the studio, it was the same thing, so we had difficulty getting agents and managers to read it, and we had difficulty getting talent to read it.

Three Kings (1999) was like that too, though less about being an unknown commodity and more about being a very polarizing one. There was a concern that Arab, Arab American, and American Muslim groups would boycott Time Warner. The filmmakers' and my views were that there are good white guys and there are bad white guys, there are good Arabs and there are bad Arabs—you can see the good and the bad in everybody. We felt it wasn't going to elicit that kind of reaction and in fact it might actually bring people together to have conversations about how we're not so different. **Training Day** (2001) and **Falling Down** (1993) also divided people.

One of the things that disappoints me about the business right now is that the idea has taken hold that a polarizing movie is not commercial. My experience has always been that there will be some people who won't go and see it, but there will be people who will be very fervent about going. And they'll convince other people to go. So that word-of-mouth, while polarizing, is more passionate. I was taught that the audience has a lot of different tastes and to presume that you can guess which one is going to be the right one is misguided. Therefore you try to do a little bit of everything because you don't know when something will be a hit. **The Perfect Storm** (2000) is a good example of that. Everybody thought it was suicide to do a $130-million movie in which everybody dies. But our feeling was that it was a great story and it was going to motivate people, and nobody else was doing that. I bet if you look at most successful movies, there's a story in each one of them about a producer who had to stick to believing in something that very few people were willing to believe along the way.

As a producer, I try to do big movies, small movies, and things in different genres. I'm working on big action franchises, I'm making a mid-budget thriller with Steven Soderbergh, and I got involved with **The Devil Inside** (2012), an under $1-million movie. I try to go with projects that stimulate my interest in some fashion, and with what makes sense on a business level. **The Devil Inside** came to me because the filmmakers had heard that I'd told people that I'd be open to doing an exorcist movie after working on **The Devil's Advocate** (1997) as an executive at Warner Bros. I'd forgotten about that until I got a call from an agent named Martin Spencer, who asked if I was still interested in an exorcist movie. I asked him to send me the script and he said the movie was already made. I wondered what he needed me for. He said they'd had a hard time selling it and would I take a look at it. I did, and thought they did a great job, but that there were some things they needed to do. I helped them recut it, brought it into Paramount and became an executive producer on the film. It was the least pressurized thing I've ever been involved in, because I didn't initiate it, and I didn't put blood, sweat, and tears into it very long. It was a really freeing experience in that way. Paramount did a great job marketing **The Devil Inside**. When I first called their head →

FOUR BROTHERS

(02–03) "I'm particularly fond of **Four Brothers** (2005), which was my first movie at Paramount," says Di Bonaventura of the Mark Wahlberg-led action ensemble about four adopted brothers who avenge their mother's death. "It was really interesting to play with the idea that family is thicker than blood. The idea that foster kids are welded every bit as strong as any genetic determination. So it was an intriguing way of looking at how we care about one another."

> "I find material for projects in various ways. There's a great team that works for my company and material will come straight from them to me. I also look at the world from a business point of view and ask what no one is doing and try to find material in that direction. I like to be a contrarian."

of marketing, Josh Greenstein, about the film, I explained that it was a little movie, but that I thought he could gross $25 million or $30 million with it. As this movie cost under $1 million, they could have a nice little profit. He agreed to see the film, along with the Paramount creative executives. Paramount eventually opened the film to $34 million, so they beat my estimate in the first weekend.

I find material for projects in various ways. There's a great team that works for my company and material will come straight from them to me. I also look at the world from a business point of view and ask what no one is doing and try to find material in that direction. I like to be a contrarian. When we got involved in **Transformers** and **G.I. Joe**, the concept of branded entertainment was there, but it was not the way it is now. Now everybody talks about it like it's the Holy Grail—which means it's time to figure out something else.

Having been a product of large studios, I understand their mechanisms. You need the big franchise movies because, not only do they generate large amounts of return when you do it right, but also because studios have so many different functions. When you do a **Training Day** or a **Four Brothers** (2005), you won't see a lot of toys or merchandise being sold. Studios have many areas that need to be fed and these big movies feed them.

Overall, I believe in the checks and balances. It's important to have a strong director, a strong producer, and a strong studio. It's dangerous if any one of those pegs gets weakened. It doesn't mean that if one is a dominant force that the movie won't come out great. But my experience of the last 20-plus years in the business is, by and large, that the best movies come out of an environment where there are healthy checks and balances. Every creative choice has been weighed, and every rock has been turned over in the search for the better idea and execution of that idea."

01 **The Devil Inside** (2012). "An under $1-million movie"

02 **The Perfect Storm** (2000), directed by Wolfgang Petersen, starring Mark Wahlberg and George Clooney

RED

(03) Di Bonaventura likes to go against the grain when it comes to selecting material for movies. When he and his cohorts were trying to set up **Red** (2010), an action movie about an aging team of black-ops agents who reunite to fight an assassin threat, his pitch focused on the potential of the underserved 35-and-older audience. "The converse argument was made to us quite a bit, which was that the demographic is too old," admits Di Bonaventura. But they persevered and were able to make the film with Summit Entertainment, with a cast including Helen Mirren, Bruce Willis, Morgan Freeman, and John Malkovich. It made nearly $200 million at the box office worldwide.

"It hit some kind of chord," he says. "It's an example of being a little bit of a contrarian. I thought, I'd love to make a movie where people under 20 will come and see it, but I fundamentally don't need them."

He credits the film's success to German director Robert Schwentke, who was able to calibrate the tonal difficulty of the film. "It's an interesting mixture of comedy and character, and violence. Multiple tones are incredibly tricky to pull off." The film also did well beyond the theatrical box office, attaining a certain kind of cult status. "What happened was a lot of the under 20-year-olds didn't see it in the theater, but they've seen it on DVD, and it's become quite a cult thing, particularly with kids in their early teens. I hear about kids seeing it with their parents. It's become sort of a family film." A sequel is in the works.

Ted Hope

"Ang Lee walked into my office one day. He had been tipped that he might win a screenplay competition in Taiwan with prize money for a production. He had asked around in New York if there was anyone who knew how to make a film for a couple of hundred thousand dollars, and I'd been recommended."

The Savages (2007)

One of the key producers to emerge from the early 1990s wave of American independent cinema, Ted Hope has shepherded nearly 70 films in his career and continues to work in the arty indie arena as the new head of the San Francisco Film Society (SFFS).

He started his career in the New Line Cinema mailroom and cut his teeth on low-budget horror films in and around New York City. The film to cement his place among the "fast-and-cheap" filmmakers set was Hal Hartley's **The Unbelievable Truth** (1989), on which Hope has a first assistant director credit. Hope went on to work on some of the most seminal indies of the decade, including Todd Haynes' **Safe** (1995), Ed Burns' **The Brothers McMullen** (1995), Nicole Holofcener's **Walking and Talking** (1996), and Ang Lee's **The Ice Storm** (1997).

Hope began his relationship with Lee on the director's early 1990s films **Pushing Hands** (1992) and **The Wedding Banquet** (1993). That time also marked the beginning of Hope's longtime partnership with producer and now Focus Features CEO James Schamus. The duo went on to found Good Machine, a production and later foreign sales company that stood among the New York indie scene's vanguard. The company was sold to Universal in 2002.

Hope, under his new production banner This Is That, continued to make films with Schamus, under a deal with Focus, and others. He has made it a habit to discover new filmmakers and went on to make multiple films with many, including Lee, Holofcener, and Todd Solondz, with whom he made **Happiness** (1998), **Storytelling** (2001), and **Dark Horse** (2011).

Among Hope's films to have collected Academy Award nominations are Tamara Jenkins' **The Savages** (2007); Todd Field's **In the Bedroom** (2001); and Alejandro González Iñárritu's **21 Grams** (2003), on which he served as executive producer. Hope also has been a prolific blogger and frequent lecturer on topics including the future of independent film and how digital delivery and social media are transforming cinema. At the SFFS, Hope will continue to shepherd filmmakers and forge new pathways for their work to be seen.

INTERVIEW

Ted Hope

" I can't say I originally set out to become a producer, but I ultimately found that my skillset translated really well to it. I was hesitant to go into film at first—I kind of felt it was self-indulgent. I thought I should try to do something that the world needed a little more. I stopped college for a while, and worked 100-hour weeks on political campaigns. To unwind I would go to the movies, rather obsessively. Along the way, when I was down about how slowly political change occurred, I applied to NYU Film School. A couple of months later, I found out I got in with a pretty decent scholarship.

I transferred into NYU undergrad in my junior year. Originally I thought I'd direct, but when I made my junior thesis project, I realized I wasn't a director. I had chased every opportunity for funding or acclaim from the school and kept co-opting my story to get the prize or the praise. I found that I had so distanced myself from what was really important to me, and I also felt that I wasn't the kind of complex storyteller that I wanted to be. That's when I realized that I could probably build greater movies and stories by finding filmmakers whose vision I admired and help facilitate getting it up on the screen.

I arrived in New York City at the time that Spike Lee, Jim Jarmusch, and the Coen brothers were all making their first films. Although the indie wave was very much building, the film schools at the time were only outfitted to teach traditional Hollywood filmmaking. There was no understanding yet of how to do things cheaper or in a different way. As I wanted to explore that, I was growing more and more frustrated with college and ultimately petitioned for my diploma early. I had had the good fortune of getting a job at New Line Cinema while I was still in school, working in the mailroom. When I was there, Janet Grillo was the head of the story department. I had dared cross the threshold from the back of the mailroom and walked up to her and said, "I'd really love to read scripts. If you let me read ten scripts I'll write up reports for you and if you like what I have to say, you're paying me." I handed in my tenth bit of coverage on the weekend that **A Nightmare on Elm Street** (1984) came out. So when I came back that next week, New Line was flush with cash and I had a part-time job reading scripts. There weren't that many people doing that yet and the whole intern side of the business had yet to be developed. You could actually get paid $25 to $100 reading scripts.

I parlayed the job at New Line into jobs with six or seven other production companies in New York. In addition to writing the coverage for the companies, I took very careful personal notes of the different scripts that I'd read and who they came from. Along the way, if a company had passed on the project, I reached out to a few writers and started developing some scripts with just sweat equity. I did that with about nine different projects and completely failed. The great thing about failing while being a producer who is just starting out is that nobody sees it. If the movie never gets made, there is no shame. It trained me to talk to writers, and I started to develop a better understanding of what people wanted, how they wanted it presented, and how

01 The Unbelievable Truth (1989), directed by Hal Hartley and on which Hope has a first assistant director credit

> "I was hesitant to go into film at first—I kind of felt it was self-indulgent. I thought I should try to do something that the world needed a little more."

to get it there. I simultaneously started working as a production assistant on low-budget horror films in the city. I was impressed by some of their techniques of how to do things cheaper and faster. It was also a sad time for production in the city—there were a lot of drugs on set and sets weren't exactly a conducive creative environment. It was a great learning experience though, in that I could look around me and see lots of mistakes being made and think about how it might have been done better. I would share the lessons I'd learned with my filmmaker friends.

Finally, one of the directors who I was working with got fed up with how long it was taking to get a film made. We had tried to get a few scripts made at that point. One day, he said to meet him at Grand Central train station. The director was Hal Hartley. He told me he was going to take me to where he grew up. On the train, he gave me the script for **The Unbelievable Truth** (1989). I was all-eager to go back and start budgeting and scheduling it, and doing every little thing I could. And he said, "No, we're actually going to shoot this one in the next five weeks. That's what you told me was all you really needed to prep a film." He and his brother and cousins had gone out and got loans for home computers, and that's the money we used to get **The Unbelievable Truth** in the can. It cost about $55,000, with 11 days of principal photography. We shot on approximately a 2:1 ratio, on 35mm. It's a film we made for almost nothing, paying everyone nothing, and had the good fortune of selling at the Toronto Film Festival to an upstart distributor, Harvey Weinstein, for more than twice it ultimately cost. But even though we got that film made, there wasn't enough yet to earn a living as a producer. Even after doing another film with Hal, **Trust** (1990), I was still working regularly as an assistant director, doing television and whatever I could to pay the bills.

Along the way, I had met James Schamus and Larry Meistrich. They were two very different guys who both wanted to move into producing, but hadn't had the physical production experience. Larry had been a PA for me on a →

02 Walking and Talking (1996), directed by Nicole Holofcener, and starring Catherine Keener and Anne Heche

"I arrived in New York City at the time that Spike Lee, Jim Jarmusch, and the Coen brothers were all making their first films."

01 **The Wedding Banquet** (1993), directed by Ang Lee

low-budget horror film. And Janet Grillo at New Line had recommended that I meet James. James was teaching at Rutgers at that point and was trying to get things made. He was also on the board of Apparatus, a short-film production company/granting organization that Christine Vachon and Todd Haynes were on the board of. I pitched both Larry and James the same idea for a company, which was Good Machine, but a much different construct than it ultimately became. They both liked the idea, but none of us had any money. And as luck would have it, James put together some money to do a short film with [French director] Claire Denis and asked me to do it with him. Part of the bonus was that we actually had six months of office overhead to start a company, and Good Machine was born. Ultimately, I went with James, and Larry went on to start the Shooting Gallery, which, along with Christine Vachon's Killer Films and Good Machine, became the New York indie production companies of the time.

I'd drawn up a list of directors who I believed in, and among them was Ang Lee. I'd seen his student films at NYU. I showed them to James,

SHE'S THE ONE
(02–04) **She's the One** (1996), starring Jennifer Aniston, Cameron Diaz, and Edward Burns. It was Burns' second film as a director and the second time he worked with Hope, who executive produced Burns' debut film **The Brothers McMullen** (1995). Both films were released by Fox Searchlight, where Hope had a long-term relationship. (02) Ted Hope with actor-filmmaker Edward Burns on set. From left to right: executive producer Michael Nozik, Hope, Burns, and cinematographer Frank Prinzi.

who thought he was great. We found out who his agent was, but he didn't want anything to do with us. Just as we finished our first production with Claire Denis, **Trust** got into the newly named Sundance Film Festival, and a film that James executive produced, Todd Haynes' **Poison** (1991), also got in. James thought maybe one of us should go to this film festival because we each had films there. I said, "Why would I want to go to a film festival? I'm going to stay in the office and do the accounting!"

When James went to Sundance, Ang Lee walked into my office one day. He had been tipped that he might win a screenplay competition in Taiwan with prize money for a production. He had asked around in New York if there was anyone who knew how to make a film for a couple of hundred thousand dollars, and I'd been recommended. He gave me two scripts he'd written: **Pushing Hands** and **The Wedding Banquet**. The next day, he found out that he had won first and second prize in the competition. Ang had spent eight years after film school basically working as a superintendent in the building he lived in and cooking meals for his wife and kids, hoping to make a movie, writing screenplays, but not getting any closer. It's amazing how well it all came together for us.

Around that time, we had an adage for how to raise funding for the movies we did, which was, "cut the budget in half." After **Pushing Hands** (1992), which had some success internationally, we thought we'd make **The Wedding Banquet** (1993) for $1.5 million. But we couldn't get any more than $700,000 in cash out of Taiwan—or anywhere else—so we cut the budget in half. We submitted the film to the Berlin Film Festival and knew enough then that we didn't want to go to →

05 **Happiness** (1998), directed by Todd Solondz

A gathering "storm"

(01–03) Part of the perfect storm that allowed 1970s Connecticut-set drama and critics darling **The Ice Storm** (1997) to get made, says Hope, is that director Ang Lee's 1995 **Sense and Sensibility** "had made over $100 million worldwide—so Ang had won the right to do something unique."

The producer's relationship with studio indie label Fox Searchlight also went a long way toward getting the $15 million adaptation of Rick Moody's novel to the screen. "We were on very good terms with Searchlight," Hope says. "We had done the first film that (Searchlight founder) Tom Rothman had distributed there: Ed Burns' **The Brothers McMullen**. We also had made a follow-up with Burns at Searchlight, **She's the One**, which was a little $3-million movie that had two (at the time) unknown actresses in it named Cameron Diaz and Jennifer Aniston, and consequently went on to make lots of money with all of its relicensing. Lindsay Law, who we had done about 15 movies with and had a great relationship with, ended up succeeding Tom at Searchlight, and **The Ice Storm** was his first production there. So we had a great environment—Tom, Lindsay, and the whole Searchlight system believed in us. Ang also was at that point where he was still incredibly hungry and having a tremendous amount of fun with experimenting and trying new things. I remember him saying that to do 1970s America and 1970s Connecticut might as well be science fiction to him because he knew so little about the period. But he was amazingly diligent in his research and notes. For every scene, he had a whole character map that had things associated with it from the time period—a painting, a song, a book, a political element. He tried to integrate all the different influences." **(03)** Hope (center) and James Schamus (right) on set.

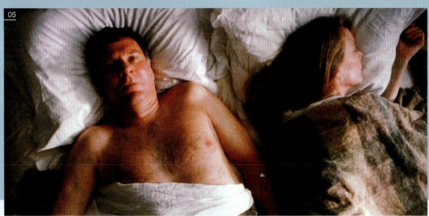

IN THE BEDROOM

(04–05) Hope says he's often faced difficult choices over financial and artistic priorities. "One of the challenges that we had at Good Machine was always the question of were we a production company that had its own sales division or were we a sales company that had its own production group? And there was no doubt that the sales company brought in far greater cash flow, though the question of what the creative community values most is certainly open to debate. There were times when tough decisions had to be made about taking a job that, initially on paper, brought in more money versus one, like all of our films, that was entirely execution-dependent. One of those cases was **In the Bedroom** (2001), a film that, at the time that we decided to go forward, was only bringing about $50,000 into the company. We also had been offered a remake of a classic horror film that we could have gotten paid full-freight producer fees on, which was significantly more. In the end, **In the Bedroom** (with a budget of just over $3 million) turned out to be a fantastic movie that got five Oscar nominations. But that type of pressure of the corporate needs versus the desire of independent producers was constantly pushing at the seams of the company."

an international festival/market without a foreign sales agent. All the sales agents said it was completely unsalable. We made a film that felt like it was from the 1940s, except that it was gay and 70 percent in Chinese. In the interim, we heard from Berlin that we'd gotten into the main competition. At the time, James and I only had $2,000 in our bank account, which we used to go to Berlin and hopefully sell the film. We were armed with just our backpacks and street smarts. Our $700,000 film did $3 million-worth of sales over the next week and a half, with James and I doing those sales on hotel room floors and bar floors or wherever we could sit down with somebody who might be a territorial buyer. Instead of taking 30 percent commission like sales agents did, we took a 10 percent commission and we took the 20 percent—next to $600,000, virtually the cost of the film—and repaid our investors, and had enough money to run our company for a couple of years.

It was clear that the business of independent film wasn't producing movies; the business was

> "It's still fun. I've almost made 70 films now, and look forward to making at least that many more—be they films or participatory-immersive-crossplatform-transmedia-experiences/data-mining-experiments."

clearly in selling the film. It seemed to me just common sense that as a production company we wanted to build our own sales company. In Berlin, I had met David Linde, who was the number two person at Miramax International at the time. You could tell that this was a really smart man who really loved film, and understood this new business in a way that very few people did. It took us two years to convince David to join us at Good Machine. We offered him something Harvey (Weinstein) couldn't give him—a third of our company, but you know a third of nothing isn't very much.

By that point, we had gotten our first overhead deal with Fox Searchlight. We had done **The Ice Storm** (1997). We were able to hire my college →

collaborator Anne Carey to run the development. Our assistants Mary Jane Skalski and Anthony Bregman had developed into first-rate producers by then and we had a company. It was a truly exciting time. You could really feel that there was business in pursuing the projects that you loved, directed by men and women of unique vision, provided that you backed it with a sound financial strategy. We got about 40-plus movies made over that period.

Then the world changed. When we started selling films directly around **The Wedding Banquet** (1993) period, there were only one or two buyers for specialty titles in each territory; it was very much a relationship business. It was supported by the television sales and an under-supplied home entertainment market. Well, television stopped buying film and the home entertainment market got saturated. The industry moved from being one that was conceived on scarcity, control, impulse buys, and mass-market focus, to one of super abundance and complete access. Now it's a much more choice-based decision-making process in terms of consumption, and requires organized, preset niches. It didn't help that economic collapse also entered into the equation. In some ways, we were all victims of the success—or, precisely, the victims of Harvey Weinstein and Quentin

"The great thing about failing while being a producer who is just starting out is that nobody sees it. If the movie never gets made, there is no shame."

Tarantino's success. Pre-**Pulp Fiction** (1994), nobody ever dreamed that you could not only get stars to be in an idiosyncratic, ambitious film like that, but that it could also go on to break $100 million domestically and similarly on an international basis. Once people started recognizing how that could be replicated to some degree, it changed the entire focus of the specialized industry to one that was based on profit margins and mass-market appeal.

Along with that, it was clear that you needed US distribution to set the value on a film. And the US distributors were hip to that fact. Consequently, the fees were coming down, making it more difficult for the company. And if you got a US distributor, they would want a piece of the international side of the action. Coming up with a solution to that wasn't easy. Around the same time, I was becoming more resolved in that I only wanted to make movies that I loved, and both David and James were itching to play in a bigger sandbox. We had several suitors for Good Machine along the way. Universal approached us with the plan to merge with USA Films and become, ultimately, what is now Focus Features. That deal was concluded really quickly.

Anne Carey and Anthony Bregman had told me that if things changed, they'd like to work for a smaller company where we weren't dictated →

01, 03 **21 Grams** (2003), starring Benicio Del Toro, Sean Penn, and Naomi Watts

02 **21 Grams** director Alejandro González Iñárritu with Benicio Del Toro

04–05 **American Splendor** (2003)

06 Hope with actor Paul Giamatti at the Los Angeles premiere of **American Splendor**

Ted Hope | Interview 69

"It was a truly exciting time. You could really feel that there was business in pursuing the projects that you loved, directed by men and women of unique vision, provided that you backed it with a sound financial strategy. We got about 40-plus movies made over that period."

by the large overheads and could crew our passion projects. We were able to construct a scenario where I got an overhead from Focus as part of the deal, and we could start the new company This Is That. We built it with the idea that we needed to make two films in the $7 million–$20 million budget range a year and we felt relatively comfortable that we could always secure those US slots to get those films made. We did that pretty well for several years. One year we actually made seven movies with just three active producers. About halfway in, Anthony decided that after 15 years it was time for him to go off on his own. And a few years later, in 2010, Anne and I realized that the period of having a production company focused on our budget range didn't make sense anymore. We made the decision first to shut down the physical office and a year later to dissolve the corporate structure itself. All of that was moving essentially to a more streamlined, fluid, flexible way of working where you could pursue a film of any budget, something as small as **Martha Marcy May Marlene** (2011), and still stay with that initial desire to pursue the movies that one loved. I think that that really becomes the essence of independent producing. But it's not easy and it requires constant change and constant adaptation.

As producers, what's required of us has increased tenfold, whereas we're rewarded with it by something that's a hell of a lot smaller in our billfold. When I first started making those movies with Hal, I wasn't supposed to do anything other than supervise the production—that's what producing was. Then we came to the point where we were really being asked to develop and package more and more material. It wasn't until I did the film **Flirt** (1995) with Hal, which was a Good Machine film, that I actually put together all the financing myself. Then in the post-**Pulp Fiction** world, we were asked to truly package it with stars, and then it got much more sophisticated—we were supposed to justify the budgets of our films. It wasn't just to have a budget, but we were asked to have foreign estimates, and do makeshift P&Ls, and nearly justify the financial plan as well as the cost of the movie.

Then we were supposed to start putting together that financial plan and bring all the pieces in together. It then got to the point where we were asked to identify the audience, start to engage the audience, build a marketing plan, and know how to deliver that marketing plan to an audience. Then, with the birth of social media and the ultimate collapse of indie film as we had known it, we're asked to aggregate our audiences, to build them, and then also to start to build our own community and start to support our own community with education, curation, things that one can do to reach and engage audiences. With that, it becomes a whole other level of tech expertise and entrepreneurship, where it is not enough to build a great movie, but I also have to start to build a platform on which it would be distributed. But if you look at the history of film, the original pioneers had to build everything themselves too, the distribution apparatus and all—but at least it was on a local basis and not on a global one.

01 Hope being interviewed at the Filmmakers Alliance Vision Awards in 2009

02 Dark Horse (2011), directed by Todd Solondz

03 Martha Marcy May Marlene (2011), directed by Sean Durkin

But…it's still fun. I've almost made 70 films now, and look forward to making at least that many more—be they films or participatory-immersive-crossplatform-transmedia-experiences/data-mining-experiments.

"I can't say I originally set out to become a producer, but I ultimately found that my skillset translated really well to it."

Marin Karmitz

"I wanted to work in cinema because I was terrible at everything else. I was useless at painting, I couldn't draw, I had a passion for architecture, but no architectural imagination, I was a very mediocre writer, and I tried acting, but was too shy."

Three Colors: Blue (1993)

Marin Karmitz is a phenomenon: one of the most prolific French producers of his generation. Alongside his production activities, he has also set up MK2, a successful distribution, exhibition, and sales company. Louis Malle, Alain Resnais, Claude Chabrol, Jean-Luc Godard—he has worked with them all. Karmitz has also branched further afield, producing movies by Iranian master Abbas Kiarostami, by great Polish director Krzysztof Kieslowski, and by American auteur Gus Van Sant.

Notable films on the producer's filmography include the **Three Colors** trilogy with Kieslowski (1993 to 1994), Chabrol's version of **Madame Bovary** (1991), Resnais' **Mélo** (1986), Kiarostami's **The Wind Will Carry Us** (1999), and Jonathan Nossiter's **Signs & Wonders** (2000). He also co-produced Van Sant's **Paranoid Park** (2007). He was associate producer on Godard's **Every Man for Himself** (1980), and his company produced Malle's classic, **Au Revoir Les Enfants** (1987).

There are several paradoxes about Karmitz. He is a figure of the 1960s, a radical leftist who fell foul of the filmmaking establishment in the turbulent post-1968 years. His directorial career was stopped in its tracks in the early 1970s and he was blacklisted. At the same time, this idealistic filmmaker with close links to the revolutionary movement proved to be an astute cinema owner and businessman. To outsiders, his filmmaking model seems akin to that of the Hollywood studios. His company is vertically integrated, handling everything from production to exhibition. He suggests his business is more in the tradition of the Lumière brothers. There is, of course, one very big difference between Karmitz and the Hollywood majors. Karmitz only produces films by auteurs.

Karmitz is nothing if not international in outlook. He came to France as a refugee. Born in 1938, Karmitz spent his early years in Romania. Once established as a producer, he has worked with filmmakers all over the world, but that leads to another surprising fact about him. He doesn't much like to travel. His passport, he says, is the cinema.

INTERVIEW

Marin Karmitz

" The role of the producer varies according to the film's content and its director. Sometimes you need to take a financial approach, sometimes you need to be more of a psychoanalyst, and at other times you need to act like a dictator. It is always essential to be competent in the different fields within cinema. This is one of the big advantages for me—I know all of the fields in the cinema world, as I have worked in them all. I know them well so I am able to react professionally. But it's not just about being professional: it's about being professional with responsibility, with authority, and with energy. I think you should be capable of dealing with every situation.

I wanted to work in cinema because I was terrible at everything else. I was useless at painting, I couldn't draw, I had a passion for architecture, but no architectural imagination, I was a very mediocre writer, and I tried acting, but was too shy. What interested me was the idea of a creative job and I ended up moving quite naturally toward the cinema. We often describe how the American studios were founded by Jewish-American immigrants (well, Jewish immigrants who later became American), and we ask why they ventured into the world of cinema. Firstly, because all of the other jobs had already been taken, whether it was banking, commerce or retail, everything had been taken and there were no vacancies left due to a vast wave of immigration. So cinema was the only remaining option. For me it was a similar state of affairs, but behind that there was another reality that took me a long time to really understand. When you are an émigré and you travel the world in search of sanctuary, everybody tells you "we don't want you." We were accepted in France, but I have always had a great fear of borders. I remember the immigrant's passport, this political refugee's passport. It was awful: we couldn't travel, we couldn't move, I was afraid. So I said to myself, I will be able to travel freely one day. I think I realized, intuitively or naturally, that the cinema would provide me with a way of traveling and of crossing borders without necessarily leaving the office. I am the only French producer (and perhaps the only producer in the world) to have made films in so many different countries throughout the world, without leaving the country. I have produced films everywhere; in Russia, in the States, in Turkey, in Latin America, in Brazil, in Japan, in China. I've produced films all over the place, without even leaving France. I have produced a lot of Iranian films, for example, and yet I have never been to Iran.

I had been an assistant director on Agnès Varda's **Cleo from 5 to 7** (1962). It was very exciting working with her—the beginning of the essential process of unlearning: a "disapprenticeship." When I was at film school, I learnt the norms of the very academic French cinema. With Varda I started to unlearn, using other ways of working; with lighter, quicker cameras and with another way of directing. And when I was on set with Varda, I met Godard, because there was a little film within Varda's film that had Godard and Anna Karina in it and it was there that I met Jean-Luc. Thanks to Varda, I became Godard's assistant.

I work almost entirely with auteurs. When you are involved with the more industrial type of cinema, you develop qualities that are more typical of someone financing a project or acting as an entrepreneur; the qualities, if you like, of a corporate manager. Personally, I can't just be a manager.

A film (**Coup pour coup**) I made as a director in 1972 had shocked a huge number of people. It was linked to the political, revolutionary movement in the aftermath of May 1968. After this film, I could no longer find work. I wanted to carry on working in cinema, as it was the only job that I knew. At this point in time the obvious solution seemed to be to do something other than direction, and I began working as a cinema owner, at the same time as being a distributor.

I initially became a cinema owner and a distributor in 1974. I had already produced my own films, working as a producer of short films, and I had been successful. I was able to use the money that I had earned producing these short

"It is the role of the producer, director, and sales representative to nurture the film and to deliver it, just as a doctor would a baby."

"Putting out the bins"

Early in his producing career, Karmitz acknowledges that he often picked up projects that others wouldn't touch. Many times, these were the most exciting projects. "Every morning I get up, pick up my bins and go downstairs to put them out on the street, near the Champs Élysées. It's an opportunity to discover what other people have put out onto the street. It's the food that has been put outside by others that I bring upstairs and choose to eat myself. This is clearly an exaggeration, but it relates to my own experience. For a very long time I was given films that nobody else wanted to produce and this is what I call putting the bins out."

films, to make my own short films. I worked as a producer only for my own films because I wasn't yet experienced enough to produce other people's films. I was therefore quite late in beginning work as a producer—I produced my first two films in 1977. The delay was also partly because I was rejected by the entire banking system. French politics between 1974 and 1980 took a pretty harsh line against anything that had once been revolutionary or that was involved with the extreme left. The political climate was rightwing and brutal, and in this context I had no credit and no access to bank credit: so I couldn't produce films. I could only begin to produce in about 1976 and I was only able to properly work as a producer when the political climate changed in France with the arrival of Mitterrand in 1981.

Jean-Luc Godard once said "le travelling est une affaire de morale." For me, production is a moral affair, and what I mean by this is that each film must find its own harmony. Because I work on prototypes, on unique subjects, I always have to adapt the economic system to suit the film's content, and at the same time adapt the film's content so that it works with the economic system. For example, I remember very clearly when I produced **Mélo** (1980) by Alain Resnais. Resnais, a well-known filmmaker both in France and throughout the world, couldn't find a producer. His agent gave me a copy of the script that everybody else had refused to work with—it was a beautiful text, but I nonetheless thought it was too long. It was a script set in the 1930s. I didn't yet know Resnais, so I asked to meet him, and I told him that I could make a certain amount of money available for his film. I think that at the time it was the equivalent of around $1.2 million—in other words it wasn't a huge amount of money. I told him I wasn't interested in searching for more money or in constantly changing my mind, giving him yeses and nos: I would rather begin working on the film. So one by one, I took each of the potential problems posed by the film script. The film could not be longer than 1 hour 45 minutes and anything beyond this would have to be cut. I proposed a →

01 Mélo (1986), directed by Alain Resnais

02 Karmitz and Alain Resnais

THREE COLORS TRILOGY

(01–04) Krzysztof Kieslowski is one of many auteurs whose films Karmitz has produced. "It was like love at first sight," Karmitz says of his first encounter with the great Polish director. Kieslowski didn't speak French, but that was no hindrance to their collaboration. Karmitz ranks Kieslowski's **Three Colors** trilogy (1993 to 1994) as one of the most complicated projects he has ever worked on—and one of the most rewarding. **(01)** Karmitz with Krzysztof Kieslowski (right).

"I wanted to make a film with Kieslowski and he said to me, 'I have a project of three films: Liberty, equality, and fraternity;' in other words a little bit of history. He had straightaway touched something that for me was incredibly important."

Humanistic vision

Karmitz has worked with several of the golden names of the French New Wave—Louis Malle, Alain Resnais, and Claude Chabrol **(05)** among them. He is adamant that, as a producer, he will only make films by auteurs he respects: "talented and gifted directors with a humanist vision." His filmography stretches to well over 70 films, but none of them, he insists, were made from the perspective of a "corporate manager" trying to turn out products. They were all labors of love. **(06) L'Enfer** (1994), directed by Chabrol. **(07) Madame Bovary** (1991), also directed by Chabrol.

solution to Resnais. This solution was to work for six weeks with the actors, rehearsing as if they were preparing for a play. The next question was whether we would film on location or in a studio. It is less expensive to shoot on location, but I also realized that Resnais worked better in the studio. We needed to work out how to minimize the costs. What was particularly expensive was renting the studio, so I suggested to Resnais that we shoot the film in just 22 days. Shooting a film in only 22 days in a studio would be a quicker process. I decided to rent the studio. So I rented it and gave Resnais two weeks before we started shooting, so that he would be able to rehearse in the studio. Right at the beginning we explained to the technicians that we didn't have a big budget. I said to them, I propose to give you the studio two weeks before shooting begins for rehearsal. I can't pay you the standard filming salary, so what would you like to do for these two weeks? The electrical technicians, the sound engineers, and the scene shifters said to me, okay, we will accept some kind of "package deal" or agree to receive a lower salary during the two weeks of rehearsal.

Jean-Luc Godard once said that the problem with production is as follows: the author writes in the script, "the forest burns." This script is then sent to the production manager and he makes →

> "I am incapable of shooting a film in a tension-filled environment. The filmmaking environment is a very stressful and demanding one that requires a positive and creative atmosphere."

a financial estimate, saying that the burning forest scene will cost $1.2 million. This total is then given to the producer who decides that it is too expensive. Whoever is in charge of finances can't get together enough money and is €1 million short. They don't try to come up with another idea and create the impression that the forest is burning, without actually burning the forest!

As far as my working with Kieslowski is concerned, there was a meeting for European film directors in Paris and I asked to see him. He came to see me. He spoke no French while I spoke no English, so we had a translator, and we spent an afternoon together talking. It was like love at first sight, like in a relationship when something happens straightaway. I wanted to make a film with him and he said to me, "I have a project of three films: Liberty, equality, and fraternity;" in other words a little bit of history. He had straightaway touched something that for me was incredibly important: the notions of liberty, equality, and fraternity together make up a story. How were we going to make it? It had become very, very interesting, because I was able to put into practice what I had learnt with Alain Resnais, Chabrol, Godard, and with all the others, and applied it to the **Three Colors** trilogy (1993 to 1994). It was very difficult to do and very complicated, as I needed to use all of my knowledge at once in order to succeed with the film. I think that if we really were successful, it was thanks to our earlier films.

With regards to Kiarostami it was a different story. An Iranian came to show me a movie from Kiarostami called **Close-Up** (1990). I didn't really know much about Iranian cinema, but I thought this film was extraordinary. I said to myself, who is Kiarostami and who is this filmmaker whom he speaks about in the film named Makhmalbaf? I had no idea who either of them were. I asked if I could meet Kiarostami, and was told yes, of course I could. So I met him and yet again it was like love at first sight. I told him I would like to produce for him, but he said he didn't need a producer as he produced himself. I would wait! We became friends and each time he came to Paris he amused me with his little personal tales. After he won the Palme d'Or (with **Taste of Cherry**, 1997) he came to Paris and every producer in the world wanted to work with him

Charlie Chaplin

(01) Alongside his producing, Karmitz has for many years run a successful sales and distribution company. He also owns his own cinemas. Despite his left-wing political activism, he runs a vertically integrated company that functions like a smaller version of a Hollywood studio. His success in re-releasing François Truffaut's films convinced Charlie Chaplin's family to choose MK2 to handle the release of restored versions of Chaplin's films. For Karmitz, Chaplin's movies have a very personal resonance. He remembers watching Chaplin's work when he was a kid in Romania. "My only memory of Romania was when I was very young. We had rented a Chaplin film and the projector caught fire!" As a refugee, building a new life in France, he identified strongly with Chaplin's stories about big-hearted outsiders.

> "Success is to make the best film possible. If we are recognized through winning awards, then that's great, but that is not the principal goal. I've received awards for films that I personally wasn't very happy with, but when I receive awards for films that I consider of a good standard, it makes me very proud."

and he said to me at that moment that we could shoot a film together. I've been doing all of his movies ever since.

Fortunately, 90 percent of the time I've been able to maintain good relations at work, but the remaining 10 percent have not been at all good. The most important moment for me is when we see the film for the first time. I attempt to watch it with an uncritical, innocent eye resembling that of a spectator. During this time, we can quickly pick up on problems. This is the most difficult and heart-wrenching part for a director and where problems tend to occur. This is where a distinction can be made between capable and less capable filmmakers. The latter deal with this stage very badly. I have deliberately chosen over the years to work with non-confrontational people. I had one very bad experience with a young director and it was hell. I am incapable of shooting a film in a tension-filled environment. The filmmaking environment is a very stressful and demanding one that requires a positive and creative atmosphere.

For me, success is to make the best film possible. If we are recognized through winning →

03 Au Revoir Les Enfants (1987), directed by Louis Malle

Collaborating with Kiarostami

Karmitz was bowled over by Abbas Kiarostami's documentary **Close-Up** (1990), about the imposter who pretends to be Kiarostami's fellow filmmaker Mohsen Makhmalbaf. "I didn't really know much about Iranian cinema, but I thought this film was extraordinary." Ironically, it was Makhmalbaf who he first started working with. It was only after Kiarostami won the Palme d'Or for **Taste of Cherry** (1997) that he and Kiarostami began their collaboration. **The Wind Will Carry Us** (1999) **(02)** marked the beginning of a creative relationship that still continues. "Every producer in the world" wanted to work with Kiarostami in this period, Karmitz remembers and he was delighted that the Iranian director chose him.

The influence of Jean-Luc Godard

As an assistant director on Agnès Varda's **Cleo from 5 to 7 (01)** in the early 1960s—one of the key early films in the French New Wave—Karmitz encountered Jean-Luc Godard (who appeared briefly in the film). He credits Godard with helping him to "unlearn" the formalist, academic approach to filmmaking that was inculcated in him at film school. Godard and Varda favored a more improvisatory approach, working with lighter, quicker cameras, using natural light and taking more risks.

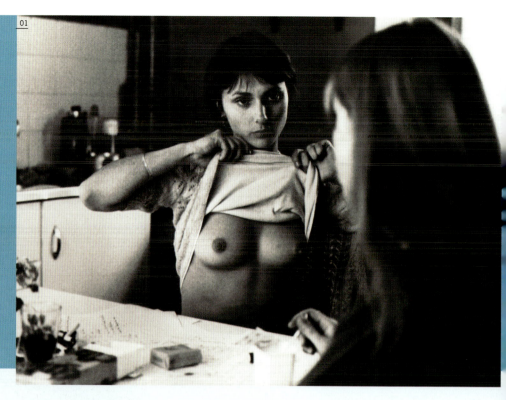

> "I asked if I could meet Kiarostami, and was told yes, of course I could. So I met him and yet again it was like love at first sight. I told him I would like to produce for him, but he said he didn't need a producer as he produced himself."

awards, then that's great, but that is not the principal goal. I've received awards for films that I personally wasn't very happy with, but when I receive awards for films that I consider of a good standard, it makes me very proud.

For a very long time I was given films that nobody else wanted to produce. In these cases the director could not find sufficient funding for the films that they wanted to have produced. This was the case for one of my first films, Louis Malle's **Au Revoir Les Enfants** (1987), and equally the case with Godard. I produced **Every Man for Himself** (1980) because no one was interested in producing it. No one had wanted to produce Louis Malle's film. Ironically, that film ended up being a worldwide success, my first success actually. I encountered huge difficulties when shooting with Chabrol; the more success I gained through working with him, the less money I actually received for my work.

It is very important to treat a film in the same way that a mother would treat her own child, as that heightens energy levels throughout the film. It is the role of the producer, director, and sales representative to nurture the film and to deliver it, just as a doctor would a baby.

There are now more than double the number of films being produced and released today than in the 1970s. Another huge change is the faster turnover of films in cinemas. In the past, films were shown on one single screen over a long period of time and were available for a year after their initial release. Today, films are issued on a huge scale for a short period of time, many disappearing after only the first week."

CERTIFIED COPY

(02–04) Certified Copy (2010) was a departure—a film made in Italy by a director [Kiarostami] who had rarely worked outside Iran. It was also partly shot in English—a language that Karmitz himself no longer speaks fluently. He is one producer who has always resisted the tyranny of the English language. **(02)** Kiarostami during filming. **(04)** Karmitz with Juliette Binoche, who starred in the film.

Marin Karmitz | Interview

LEGACY

David O. Selznick

Best known for his epic achievement **Gone with the Wind** (1939), producer David O. Selznick left his mark as an exacting perfectionist whose taste and attention to detail made him one of Hollywood's best and most dogmatic moviemakers.

His preferred method of communication was the memo. Selznick started penning missives as a teenager, while working for his father's film distribution company on the East Coast. The memorandum became a way for the young Selznick to get his point across with clarity and authority. That method stuck as he ascended through the ranks in Hollywood in the following years.

Selznick moved West in the mid 1920s, and spent about two years at MGM, then three at Paramount, and another two each at RKO and MGM, before forming his own production company, Selznick International.

Selznick started his studio career by negotiating his way into a job as a script reader at MGM on the basis of a two-week trial. He quickly proved himself, moving from the story department to producing films at the studio. He began with Tim McCoy Westerns, because the producer who'd been in charge of Westerns at the studio had grown sick of them. Wanting to make his mark, Selznick knew he had to do something that would turn heads. He'd recognized the formulaic nature of Westerns and decided to produce two films simultaneously for about the price of one. He was successful, but ultimately got fired after a fierce disagreement with Irving Thalberg, who oversaw production at MGM at the time.

Selznick moved to Paramount under studio head B.P. Schulberg, where he would again prove himself within two weeks. He came up with a new system for writers and producers, dreamt up new titles for films that required them, and inundated the studio's executives with his persistent memos. Selznick gained power and position, but after a few years started to feel strongly that the studio's assembly-line approach was not the way forward. He was given an opportunity to run production at RKO, and made several films there that stood out for their strong female characters, from **A Bill of Divorcement** (1932) to **Little Women** (1933)—

01 Selznick on the set of **Gone with the Wind** (1939)

02 Selznick with Vivien Leigh, Victor Fleming, Carole Lombard, and Clark Gable (1939)

> "An exacting perfectionist whose taste and attention to detail made him one of Hollywood's best and most dogmatic moviemakers."

both starring Katharine Hepburn and directed by George Cukor.

While at Paramount, Selznick had married Irene Mayer, the daughter of MGM chief Louis B. Mayer. When in 1933 Selznick got an offer to re-join MGM to make films from his own perch, he moved back. He tackled literary adaptations **David Copperfield**, **A Tale of Two Cities**, and **Anna Karenina** (all 1935), which were among his most challenging pictures there. Despite his achievements at MGM, he was haunted by the implications of nepotism. It was whispered around Hollywood that "the son-in-law also rises"—a rather unfair assessment of a man who had already risen so auspiciously on his own merits.

In 1935, Selznick finally launched his own company, Selznick International, with Thalberg serving as one of his first investors. Under that banner, he made **The Prisoner of Zenda** and **A Star Is Born** (1937), and his back-to-back Best Picture Oscar winners: **Gone with the Wind** and Alfred Hitchcock's **Rebecca** (1940). Selznick fought and willed his pictures to life. A couple of weeks into shooting **Gone with the Wind**, he replaced director Cukor with Victor Fleming. He

also had his creative battles with Hitchcock, with whom he didn't make a second film until 1945's **Spellbound**.

As his memos revealed, Selznick was detail obsessed. He fixated on the eyebrow shape of his leading ladies Ingrid Bergman and Vivien Leigh, and fretted over Clark Gable's wardrobe. "I am interested in the thousands and thousands of details that go into the making of a film," he had said in 1957. "It is the sum total of all these things that either makes a great picture or destroys it. The way I see it, my function is to be responsible for everything."

After his Oscar and box-office successes, Selznick was forced to liquidate his company for tax reasons. He continued to make a few films under David O. Selznick Productions, including **Duel in the Sun** (1946), starring his second wife Jennifer Jones.

Selznick died in 1965 at the age of 63. His name lives on today through the Producer's Guild of America's David O. Selznick Achievement Award, which honors a producer's body of work in motion pictures.

03 Anna Karenina (1935)
04 Rebecca (1940)
05 Gone with the Wind (1939)

Kees Kasander

 "As a producer, you raise the money, develop the script, do everything. Then you hand it over to the director. Sometimes, we spend three to four years developing a film into something that is interesting for the market. You need to be supported for that work, not hated for it."

The Pillow Book (1996)

Kees Kasander's producing career has been dominated by his collaboration with a single filmmaker—the British director Peter Greenaway. Kasander first became aware of Greenaway's work in the early 1980s and was smitten. The moment of epiphany came when he saw a Greenaway retrospective at the Edinburgh Film Festival and recognized a director whose preoccupations matched his own. Within reason, the Dutch producer will do anything he can to help Greenaway realize his artistic vision. At a time when British broadcasters and public funders have largely spurned Greenaway, Kasander has enabled him to go on working.

Kasander started working with Greenaway on **A Zed & Two Noughts** (1986) and the two have subsequently made **Drowning by Numbers** (1988), **The Cook, the Thief, His Wife, and Her Lover** (1989), **Prospero's Books** (1991), **The Baby of Mâcon** (1993), **The Pillow Book** (1996), **8½ Women** (1999), **The Tulse Luper Suitcases** (2003), and **Nightwatching** (2007), among other audiovisual work. The bond between the producer and Greenaway remains as strong as ever. At the time of the interview, work was almost complete on Greenaway's new feature, **Goltzius and the Pelican Company**, and Kasander was already beginning to crank up Greenaway's next project, **Food for Love** (an adaptation of Thomas Mann's *Death in Venice*).

Alongside his films with Greenaway, the producer has a very successful parallel career. The Kasander Film Company, based in Rotterdam, specializes in making kids' movies, documentaries, and multimedia work and exhibitions.

Kasander has also worked with plenty of other directors with strong personal visions too, among them Andrea Arnold (**Fish Tank**, 2009); Sophie Fiennes (**The Pervert's Guide to Cinema**, 2006; **Over Your Cities Grass Will Grow**, 2010); Larry Clark (**Ken Park**, 2002); Paul Tickell (**Christie Malry's Own Double-Entry**, 2000), and Ben Sombogaart (**Crusade in Jeans**, 2006).

INTERVIEW

Kees Kasander

"I produce in two ways. If I produce a Peter Greenaway film, I produce a Peter Greenaway film. I have to make the film he has in mind. It's not like I try to make a Kasander production out of a Greenaway film. That doesn't make sense. The strong point for that sort of cinema is Greenaway. I have to try to understand what he would like to do or help him make that film work. If I am not doing a Greenaway film, then the role of the producer is much bigger. It needs to be a Kasander production.

If a director is not like Greenaway or Lars von Trier, then the producer should be in charge. That's my feeling after 30 years. Somebody needs to be in control of the film. In the case of Peter Greenaway, I need to support his view and his film. In another case, if I make a family film, I need to be the driving force. Either you support the vision [of the director] and the filmmaking and the style or you make something for a large audience.

Working at the Rotterdam Film Festival with its founder Hubert Bals was the perfect way to start in the film business. Hubert Bals was very stimulating. There were only four of us. We had to do everything ourselves. Hubert had very good taste in films, one that was auteur-driven. I started as head of distribution and then I became producer of the festival. Sometimes in the festival, there were directors who wanted to make their next films. Raoul Ruiz came to me and said, "I want to make a film in Patagonia. Are you interested?" I said Patagonia is a long way off, but if you want to do something here, in this neighborhood, then I am happy to do it. We made that film, **On Top of the Whale** (1982). That was my starting point. I learned everything from that film.

We decided on one location and that was the house of Dickie Parlevliet—who also worked for the festival. We had Henri Alekan as the DoP. He had done **Beauty and the Beast** (1946) for Jean Cocteau and was from the old French school. He knew a lot about glass paintings and so we used glass paintings. It was a great time. The total budget was $45,000. We shot the film in 13 days. There were 18 takes. He [Ruiz] used almost all of the material [he shot] in order to make the film.

I found out by doing that film that I had some producing skills. There is not a school for becoming a film producer. I never, never had the idea that I would become a producer. As a producer, you need to be able to sort out a million problems under pressure. You need a special brain for that. My father had a similar kind of brain. He was a foreman in a factory in Holland. I think I inherited that brain from him. He can solve a lot of problems under pressure. He had a very logical and very quick mind. That's something you need as a producer—you need to be quick. I try to stay away from the shooting as much as possible and keep an overview of the film. I think a producer is the only one who can look at the rushes. A director looks at the rushes completely differently from anybody else. A production designer looks at his production design. A cameraman looks at his camerawork. I try to look at the film—and I try to stay at a distance.

At some point, I heard a rumor from the UK

01 Drowning by Numbers (1988), directed by Peter Greenaway

Guiding Greenaway to greener pastures

(02) **The Draughtsman's Contract** (1982) was an unlikely popular success in the UK. It was funded by the British Film Institute and Channel 4, and brought the work of Greenaway—then best known for experimental short films like **Dear Phone** (1976), **The Falls** (1980), and **H Is for House** (1973)—to a much wider audience. It was sumptuously shot, with the 16th century recreated in loving detail. The plot contained both eroticism and intrigue. It played at film festivals all over the world and won Greenaway an international reputation. Kees Kasander was one of the many who saw it on the festival circuit. Soon afterward, the Dutchman began producing for the English director. In the intervening 25 years, Greenaway's work has come in and out of fashion, but it has rarely been easy to find financing for his films, especially in the UK. "I always tell Peter that if you want to be popular in the UK, you have to die first," Kasander jokes affectionately.

that this film, **The Draughtsman's Contract** (1982), was a very interesting film. Edinburgh at that time organized a retrospective of Peter Greenaway's work. I went there to see if it was interesting for Rotterdam. I spent a week there seeing all the shorts and **The Falls** (1980) and **The Draughtsman's Contract**. I've always said that if I was a filmmaker, then I would make films like that. They were very close to my personal taste. I invited Peter to come to Rotterdam. Peter came to Rotterdam with his film and then he went to the zoo in Rotterdam. He said to me, "You're producing films here. Can we not shoot in Rotterdam?" That's how it happened. Peter then made **A Zed & Two Noughts** (1986), partly set in Rotterdam Zoo.

It's a two-way street with Peter. He will ask for something and I will give him something else. We have a very interesting way of communicating. He sometimes asks for impossible things. He says, "I would like this, but I am sure it is impossible." We then turn it into something that is possible. It's not like he is demanding. It is really teamwork. I try to get as much as possible for him for the money that is available. He knows he needs to be flexible as well. With the help of the DoPs we are using, especially Reinier van Brummelen, we always come up with something interesting.

The Cook, the Thief, His Wife and Her Lover (1989) was not financed at all in the UK. They didn't like it. They hated the script. It was turned down by Channel 4, it was turned down by British Screen, it was turned down by everybody. The film was made with money from outside the UK, but shot in the UK. It helped because we could get the cast we wanted. But that gives you an idea that there was never really a lot of support for Peter's work while he was living there. I always tell Peter that if you want to be popular in the UK, you have to die first. It was the same with Powell and Pressburger! It's not just the English. Many →

> "People always have this idea that because you are making one film every year or two years that it is a very big source of income. It is not. There is basically no interest in art-house cinema. It has become less and less and less."

> "There are actors who like working with Peter and actors who don't. With Peter, you need to trust yourself as an actor—and then you're fine."

nationalities have a problem with supporting their own talent. Look at Michael Haneke. He became popular because he moved to Paris.

Peter moved to Amsterdam. Maybe there will be a revival in the UK soon, but he is not very popular there at all, not to financiers. The UK has always supported a different kind of filmmaking. Look at Ken Loach. He didn't work for ten years in the UK. Now, Europe has discovered him and Europe is putting money behind him.

I set up the first Kasander Film Company in 1983–84 with Peter. The idea was that a film always had to be able to get into a big festival. That was the benchmark when I started. I was like a publisher. I wanted to publish/produce films that were of a quality so that ten years, 20 years from now, they'd still be around.

I was never able to pre-sell the films. I had to start every time from scratch. Even now, when I start financing a Greenaway film—and we are now on number 13 together—I have to start from scratch. In those early years, it was very difficult because you had to do some more commercial films in order to support the Greenaway films. People always have this idea that because you are making one film every year or two years that it is a very big source of income. It is not. There is basically no interest in art-house cinema. It has become less and less and less. You have to defend yourself at a certain moment, when Peter is not very popular, as to why you are making Greenaway films.

Nothing has changed [in the relationship with Peter] other than that we've moved more to post-production. That is a big change. Peter is also a painter and he is somebody who understands how to use post-production in a different way. A long time ago, he did a series called **A TV Dante** (1989). This was his first exercise in post-production. If you look at **Goltzius and the Pelican Company**, the film we are just finishing, it is exactly the same, but of course the technology is much more advanced. In terms of making digital films, Peter has been a front-runner and I have always supported that.

There are actors who like working with Peter and actors who don't. With Peter, you need to trust yourself as an actor—and then you're fine. Martin Freeman in **Nightwatching** (2007) was fantastic. He was doing what he thought was good. He had a lot of self-confidence. I liked his performance enormously. Gielgud, in **Prospero's Books** (1991), was Sir John! He came on set and everybody was silent. That man had such presence that everything was clear there. It was his idea, **Prospero's Books**. He had wanted to do *The Tempest*. He started the whole thing. He was in **A TV Dante** and got to know Peter. That was a fantastic experience.

If you are 30 years old in Hollywood, there is not that much interesting work. F. Murray Abraham [who is in Goltzius] said, "I really want to do this because I have been in so many silly films of late. This is a good ending of a career." That's the way actors look at it—either do something that makes you lots of money or do something interesting.

My company was based on a long relationship with Peter. We decided to go with each other until one of us was fed up with the other one. What I invented for our company was family →

01 Prospero's Books (1991), directed by Greenaway and starring John Gielgud

THE COOK, THE THIEF, HIS WIFE AND HER LOVER

(02–03) Gluttony, cannibalism, and incest were all thrown into the melting pot for Greenaway's 1989 film, **The Cook, the Thief, His Wife and Her Lover**. Producer Kasander took it all in his stride, even if British financiers didn't. "**The Cook, the Thief, His Wife and Her Lover** was not financed at all in the UK. They didn't like it. They hated the script. It was turned down by Channel 4, it was turned down by British Screen, it was turned down by everybody," the producer recalls. "The film was made with money from outside the UK, but shot in the UK—and the only reason we were shooting it in the UK was because Peter wanted to be in England." **(02)** Helen Mirren with Peter Greenaway on set.

Greenaway, all the way

(01–04) Whether asked to provide animals from Rotterdam Zoo (**A Zed & Two Noughts (04)**), work with one of Britain's greatest Shakespearian actors (John Gielgud in **Prospero's Books (01)**), put together a co-production with Japan (**The Pillow Book**), pay homage to Fellini (**8½ Women (02)**), invoke the spirit of Rembrandt (**Nightwatching (03)**), or organize the logistics for a film about three women from different generations all drowning their husbands (**Drowning by Numbers**), Kasander has always found a way to help Greenaway realize his vision.

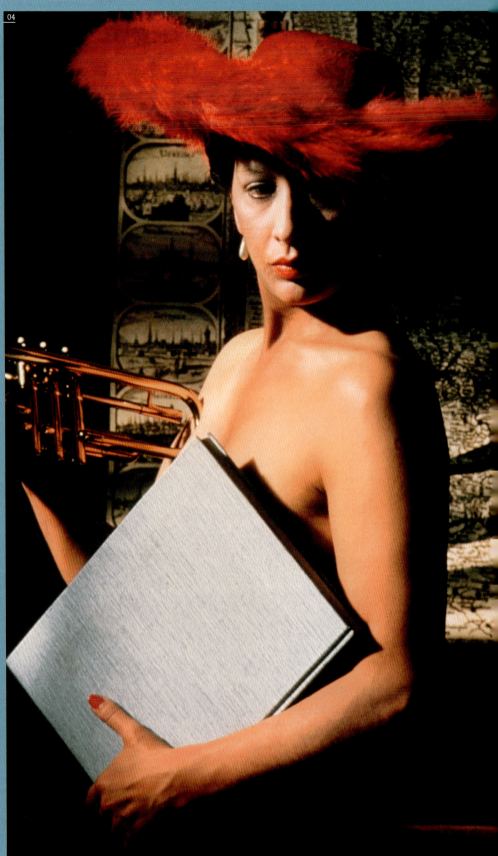

> "As a producer, you need to be able to sort out a million problems under pressure. You need a special brain for that."

films in Holland. There is this great spot at Christmas when the whole family goes to the cinema. That's the only time in the year really. I started making films for them [the Dutch family audience] as a counterpart to my work with Peter. The turnover in that Christmas period can be enormous. In two or three weeks, you make more admissions than at any other time of the year. It's 40 percent of the year's turnover—only family films work at that time. They don't travel very well, though.

As for co production, I always used to say that in Holland, we have an advantage—we don't have a market and so we have to go out. I always had to travel to all the places where there was a possible source of money for a new film with Peter. I ended up in Japan, China, Hong Kong, Argentina—everywhere there could be money available for our films. I took a plane a week or a train. I like Rotterdam (where my company is still based), but I have never been in an office anyway because we are always shooting somewhere else. I spent more time outside Holland than inside Holland. I like to see myself more as a European producer, not as a Dutch producer. Most of my films aren't in Dutch, they are in English.

Ken Park (2002) had been a dead project for seven years. It was written by Harmony Korine and was a fantastic script, but was owned by Larry Clark and Ed Lachman. I brought Larry and Ed together again and said you have to make this film. I got money from France and we shot the film on 35mm near Los Angeles. I always felt it was an important film. It was a film about the most important period in your life—adolescence—and nobody was making films about that at that time. I felt this was perfect. Of course, Larry was not easy and it was a complicated project. There was no known cast. All the kids were from the streets. It's not easy, but it's a good film. At that time, I was more popular because of **Ken Park** than because of Peter.

For me, the most important thing is to make the films. I have no control over distribution. Distributors can change overnight. When we opened **The Cook, the Thief, His Wife and Her Lover**, we opened at the Lumiere. That was an 800-seater. It was packed every night. For six long weeks it was sold out every day. You couldn't imagine that any more. Times have changed and everyone stays home.

The next step is to get ourselves organized distribution-wise, but it needs to be internet-based. The cinema is not good for art house any more. There is a big audience all over the world (for a Greenaway film), but you can't reach them any more because the distribution system is not working for us. You have to reach them in a different way.

The festivals have become like theme parks and they are not a guide for audiences. There are lots of parties for the filmmakers. I am not a party person. If you work four years on a film, and your film is squeezed in with 499 other films at a festival, it's not nice, I can tell you. If you are in Cannes, you are at least popular for two hours. In Toronto, you are popular for two seconds! That's not worth it, all this work. I haven't felt tempted to direct myself. Peter is so much better than I am. I had better support someone who is really good!

I've hardly ever been a minority co-producer. I was soon a very well-known producer because of **The Cook, the Thief, His Wife and Her** →

05 Ken Park (2002), directed by Larry Clark

> "It's funny how, as soon as the film is financed, all sorts of mechanisms start working against the producer. Of course, there are many, many bad producers in the world, but there are also many, many bad financiers."

Lover and I'd get a script a week. Basically, I took the ones I liked and produced them. How do I choose them? They have to be good for Cannes or Venice, projects with a strong signature, or they need to be good for Christmas time in Holland. The rest I won't pursue. I can spot it [a script with a strong signature] from a million miles. There are not that many good projects in the world.

On Andrea Arnold's **Fish Tank** (2009), I had a very bad experience. The UK Film Council took over and because I was a foreigner, they tried to push me out. They are people who are supposed to give you money, not produce themselves. I had to fight them, but you can't win that battle. It's normal. The UK has always been like this. There is no difference between the UKFC at that time or Channel 4 in the 1970s or British Screen. They were behaving exactly the same. You can't expect directors to stand by producers. Directors want to make their films. Some are working for years on their film. You can't blame it on the filmmakers. You have to blame it on the financiers. They should give the money to the producer so the producer can spend it on the film. Over the years, there are many, many producers who've given up basically because they can't stand this anymore. As a producer, you raise the money, develop the script, do everything. Then you hand it over to the director. Sometimes, we spend three to four years developing a film into something that is interesting for the market. You need to be supported for that work, not hated for it. It's funny how, as soon as the film is financed, all sorts of mechanisms start working against the producer. Of course, there are many, many bad producers in the world, but there are also many, many bad financiers. My biggest struggle is still with these mechanisms.

01 Over Your Cities Grass Will Grow (2010), directed by Sophie Fiennes

01

The perils of international co-production

(02–03) "On Andrea Arnold's **Fish Tank** (2009), I had a very bad experience," Kasander recalls. "They [the British funders] took over and because I was a foreigner, they tried to push me out. They are people who are supposed to give you money, not produce themselves. I had to fight them, but you can't win that battle." After many years of being rebuffed by British financiers while working with Greenaway, Kasander is phlegmatic about his difficult time on **Fish Tank**. It's one of the perils of international co-production that you'll rub up against partners with different attitudes toward producing than your own. Nonetheless, he makes it clear that he wants to be the lead producer and also to work with directors like Arnold who have a "strong signature" and whose films will contend for berths at the major international festivals.

Jon Kilik

"I just want to make the films I want to make with the people I want to make them with, and be able to give the directors the help they need. And, at the same time, find partners—whether they are studios, independents, foreign distributors or private investors—who will back us. I've been able to pull it off so far."

Babel (2006)

Jon Kilik's willfully independent producing ethos found its roots in the early 1980s American New Wave of filmmakers that included Jim Jarmusch and the Coen brothers. While Kilik worked on the more traditional New York sets of Martin Scorsese and Sidney Lumet, his indie spirit persisted. After gaining his first full producer stripes on a low-budget feature (1988's **The Beat**), Kilik began a long-term relationship with Spike Lee, starting with the director's **Do the Right Thing** (1989), and his early 1990s films **Mo' Better Blues**, **Jungle Fever**, and **Malcolm X**, to his more recent films, such as **Inside Man** (2006).

Along the way, he's produced a number of notable directorial debuts, including Robert De Niro's **A Bronx Tale** (1993), Julian Schnabel's **Basquiat** (1996), Gary Ross' **Pleasantville** (1998), and Ed Harris' **Pollock** (2000). Kilik has continued to collaborate with most of his directors, such as Schnabel, with whom he's made four additional films, including the Oscar-nominated **The Diving Bell and the Butterfly** (2007). All were produced outside of the Hollywood system. He juggles smaller indies—Jarmusch's **Broken Flowers** (2005)—and larger, ultimately studio-distributed films—Oliver Stone's **Alexander** (2004) and Alejandro González Iñárritu's **Babel** (2006)—with aplomb.

And even when he's producing what, on the surface, looks like a studio project, such as **The Hunger Games** (2012), Kilik prefers to maintain his independent stance. Studio perks have never lured him—he still proudly carries his own tattered Blackberry.

In addition to **The Hunger Games** films, Kilik continues to develop projects with filmmakers including Sean Penn, Lee, Schnabel, and De Niro.

INTERVIEW

Jon Kilik

"I grew up in Millburn, New Jersey, and went to the University of Vermont in Burlington, Vermont. I majored in political science, but also took film classes. It was through the inspiration of film-production and film-criticism professors that the switch flipped on and I got interested in filmmaking. But those broad education roots were really important. I was glad I had the English, political science, and sociology background that fed the human, social, and political storytelling that I was always attracted to when I was a moviegoer and that inspired me to become a moviemaker. Those were the kinds of stories that I wanted to try to pursue.

After I graduated from UVM, I moved to New York to continue to make the type of films that I started in Burlington. I had a group of friends who were all the same age and in the same boat. We worked on our own scripts and workshopped things together. It is so important to stay connected with your network—your peers who have the same passion for filmmaking and the same amount of time available—so you can team up. It's crucial to have people who can go into battle with you. That is really 99 percent of it. You've got to dig in and be super persistent, super passionate, and fight your way through, whether you're making your first film or later in your career. None of it just happens, it doesn't come to you. You have to learn to be strong, aggressive, and work on your skills: How to pitch a story and how to work with writers, actors, directors and the crew, while also dealing with the financing, the studios, and all of the outside elements that will help you get your movie made.

When I moved to New York in 1979, I was doing two things that were kind of on parallel tracks. One was developing scripts and trying to find financing for projects with friends from high school and college, and with people who I met through work who shared the same dream. There was also my day job, which was working on the sets of features. I don't come from a family with movie connections. I was lucky to fall in with a great group of people who took me under their wing. I got a job as a production assistant and worked my way up to location scout, location manager, and assistant director. At that time, in the early 1980s, New York was so busy and alive. Woody Allen, Sidney Lumet, Alan Pakula, and Martin Scorsese were making movies almost every year. Being on those sets right after college was the ultimate graduate program for me. Woody's **Stardust Memories** (1980), Lumet's **The Verdict** (1982), Scorsese's **The King of Comedy** (1983), Pakula's **Sophie's Choice** (1982) were the movies that gave me my start. When you're given that opportunity, you have to go the extra mile. It meant a lot of seven-day weeks and a lot of personal sacrifice.

If you want to continue to grow and get better at anything, you have to put in the time. Back then, I might have been starting out as a PA, but I was always looking over the shoulder of the DoP or the production designer or the costume designer, and quietly watching the actors and director. I was building a second network with people who were at the top of their field, but also exchanging ideas and asking questions and wondering what goes into their work. I was

01 Do the Right Thing (1989), written and directed by Spike Lee

02 Malcolm X (1992), directed by Lee and starring Denzel Washington

03 Mo' Better Blues (1990), also directed by Lee and starring Washington

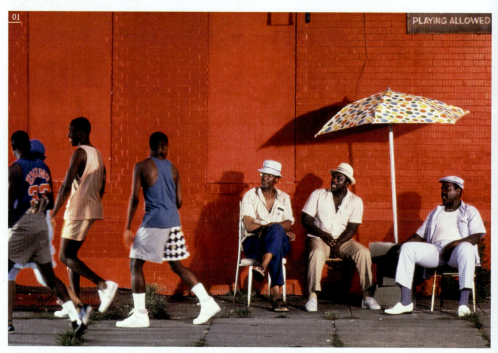

> "I don't come from a family with movie connections. I was lucky to fall in with a great group of people who took me under their wing."

planting the seeds for producing. You have to know what's behind the thoughts of a cameraman, a production designer, a costume designer, and everybody on your crew. It's not just script development and casting, even though those are two of the most important things.

After about seven years of building experience on sets, the two worlds came together when one of my projects finally got financed. A friend of mine from high school, Paul Mones, and I had developed his script called **The Beat** and we convinced Vestron Pictures to make it in 1986. At that point, I had just AD-ed for the Coen brothers on **Raising Arizona** (1987) and I was John Huston's production supervisor on **Prizzi's Honor** (1985). I had a pretty good handle on how to run a movie set. What also paid off was my seven years of development experience—working on scripts, working with writers, writing myself, doing off-off Broadway theater with our own material, going to Los Angeles every chance I got, taking our scripts around to the agencies, and trying to get financing at the mini independents—plus all of the rejections that happened along the way.

We got our big break thanks to the video revolution, when companies started to look to lower-budget, independent films as product that could feed the new ancillary markets of cable and VHS. Smaller, independent companies started up to feed the need for this extra material. You could get a couple of hundred thousand dollars and make your own movie. It gave an opportunity to the guys who started the 1980s American independent New Wave: John Sayles made **Return of the Secaucus Seven** (1979), Jim Jarmusch made **Stranger Than Paradise** (1984), Ethan and Joel Coen made **Blood Simple** (1984), then Spike Lee made **She's Gotta Have It** (1986).

The Beat (1988) was about tough kids in a poor, urban neighborhood who are inspired by the good-guy English teacher. We did all the things that I learned on the big movies, just on a smaller scale. We got the DoP (Tom DiCillo) who shot **Stranger Than Paradise** for Jim, and the composer (Carter Burwell) who wrote the music

for Ethan and Joel for **Blood Simple**. We started to cast it and showed the people at Vestron that we could make it on a low budget. Vestron had bought a library and had some success with their VHS sales, but they were running out of material so they had to find their own; and they wanted to move into theatrical releasing. They greenlit three films that year: **The Beat**, Abel →

Jon Kilik | Interview

> "You've got to dig in and be super persistent, super passionate, and fight your way through, whether you're making your first film or later in your career."

Ferrara's **China Girl**, and their one big hit, **Dirty Dancing**. Our movie ended up being released theatrically for a couple of weeks, but it was not a commercial success. I had to figure out what to do next, either go back to being a production supervisor, AD or continue to develop my own projects with Paul. We ended up doing three movies together. None of them found commercial success, but we forced them into existence. You've got to get your movie made. If you don't get your movie made, you're doing something wrong. If you can get it made, you've really achieved something, whether the movie succeeds or not is the next part of the challenge. Getting that first one done was a big deal.

Right around the time **The Beat** was released, I met Spike Lee. He was editing **School Daze** (1988), but he already had his eyes on his next one. He was working on an early draft of **Do the Right Thing** (1989). David Picker, who was running Columbia and was financing **School Daze**, told Spike about me and we met in January 1988. Spike wanted to come back to New York and shoot a film that was in the spirit of his independent film-school style with people he knew and was comfortable working with. But he also knew that at the next level you have to deal with the unions and a structure that isn't the same as when you make a movie for $100,000. I had made movies in the more traditional way and I'd also made a low-budget indie film. Spike wanted to blend those things together. We immediately hit it off. Spike and I are less than three months apart in age, grew up Knicks fans, and both have the same kind of fight in us. He gave me an early draft of **Do the Right Thing** and I read it and loved it. It wasn't financed and he didn't even have an agent. He was working on it in his little apartment, hammering it out while finishing **School Daze**. He said, "I want to go to Paramount, get $10 million, get Robert De Niro, and shoot next June." The long story short, we didn't get the first three things, but we started shooting in June. We simply wouldn't quit—even when Paramount passed, when Robert De Niro passed, and when there wasn't anybody out there who would give us anything close to $10 million. On top of that, Spike wanted total creative control and wanted to shoot it in the real location in Brooklyn. We let our obstacles guide us, not get us down. We never compromised the work itself. We could compromise the budget, we could adjust the casting ideas. We ended up making the movie at Universal for $6 million, with Danny Aiello. →

01 **Pollock** (2000), directed by and starring Ed Harris

"None of it just happens, it doesn't come to you. You have to learn to be strong, aggressive, and work on your skills."

02 **Before Night Falls** (2000), directed by Julian Schnabel and starring Javier Bardem and Johnny Depp

03 **The Diving Bell and the Butterfly** (2007), the French language film directed by Schnabel

04 **Basquiat** (1996), directed by Schnabel and starring Jeffrey Wright

Building Babel

(01–04) The multi-lingual, multi-narrative **Babel** (2006) came together in an unusual way. Kilik, director Alejandro González Iñárritu, and their partners (including producer Steve Golin and then-agent John Lesher) ultimately ended up making the film they wanted to make, despite the myriad obstacles. "We all said we'd work on it together and worry later about who was going to finance it or where to find a home for it," Kilik remembers. "We never found a home, actually, we just ended up selling off separate territories. People we'd show it to would say the script was good, that they respected Alejandro and would love to be in business with him. But it was set in three countries and in five languages—and maybe they'd give us $12 million. We figured we needed a little more than that, so we held out. We kept financing the development and scouting ourselves. Then CAA said they had a client who was interested: Brad Pitt. He was going to be a great help with the financing, but we had to decide if it was right for the script. It was not a movie star's movie. It was an ensemble with a delicate balance to it. You have to serve the story and be responsible to what is the best way to make your movie. Brad said he'd do whatever it took. He just wanted to make the film and help realize Alejandro's vision. He was just unbelievably supportive and generous, without any vanity or ego. Holding out for a bigger budget [about $28 million] was a really important decision. We needed the extra time for sequences like the night club in Tokyo or when Brad carries Cate Blanchett to the helicopter. These are scenes that are maybe an eighth of a page in the script, but they have a hundred shots each in them, and you can't pull them off if you don't have the money to spend two or three days shooting. The film needed the texture and that cinematic side that only comes with the extra time. We fought hard for that and we got it by virtue of having a great partner in Brad. That's what elevated the movie. If we'd shot that movie in 40 days instead of 100 days, it would have been a totally different film."

(02) Kilik on set in Mexico in 2005. **(03)** Director Alejandro González Iñárritu (center) celebrates with Kilik (left) and Steve Golin (second left), and Paramount CEO Brad Grey after winning the award for Best Dramatic Motion Picture for **Babel** at the 64th Annual Golden Globe Awards in Los Angeles, 2007.

Frequent collaborators

(05–06) Kilik stresses the importance of cultivating relationships with creatives and executives in the film business. He has long-term, ongoing conversations with directors and writers, many of which have yielded multiple collaborations. One key example is screenwriter Gary Ross, whose first movie as a director, **Pleasantville** (1998), was produced by Kilik. Almost 15 years later, they again teamed up for **The Hunger Games** (2012). "Gary and I met in 1997 and set off to make **Pleasantville**," says Kilik. "After that, we kept in touch and kept talking about different stories. He would send me various original scripts that he was writing, as we were looking for something to do together. The projects that he and I were talking about doing were all his own homegrown ideas, like **Pleasantville**. He heard about **The Hunger Games** through his kids. He read the book and told me, 'Jon you have to read this, I really think this is what I should do next and I'm going to try to get you on board with me.' He did. [Producer] Nina Jacobson had the rights to the book. Gary met with Nina when she was looking to attach a director. It was an open directing job, which is not typical of what Gary looks for. I had met Nina in 1998 and worked with her two or three times when she was the president of production at Disney on a couple of Spike Lee's films and a movie directed by Tim Robbins. She knew me and trusted me. Gary and I had already made one movie together and now faced the challenge of how to pull off this one. You never know when or how people may come back into your life. It was a great partnership for the three of us. Who would have guessed?"

> "You have to know what's behind the thoughts of a cameraman, a production designer, a costume designer, and everybody on your crew. It's not just script development and casting, even though those are two of the most important things."

DEAD MAN WALKING

(01) Tim Robbins shared with Kilik his desire to direct on the set of Spike Lee's **Jungle Fever** (1991), in which Robbins had a small part. Though **Bob Roberts** (1992) became Robbins' directorial debut, the two eventually made **Dead Man Walking** (1995) together, as well as 1999's **Cradle Will Rock**. Robbins' then-spouse Susan Sarandon had received the book through her agent, and it became a natural project for them to start working on. They found a backer in independent distributor PolyGram.

Sometimes you can make a better movie when you don't get your first-choice actor, budget or studio—and in this case, that's what happened. The success of **Do the Right Thing** was a big breakthrough for both of us. We kept making movies together, although I chose not to become part of his company because I wanted to continue to have my own independent career. I started to option material or get involved very early with new projects. I always went with my gut on what to do and who to be involved with. It was very personal for me, it was never about a job, and it was always about the relationship with the person—the director or writer, and the story we wanted to tell. I trust my instincts, whether it's making a movie about the art world in New York City in the 1980s with Julian Schnabel, or living on the Pine Ridge Indian Reservation and making a film about a Native American family with Chris Eyre (2002's **Skins**). Those are stories that struck me, which I just liked. I wanted to go on those journeys.

I've produced a lot of directorial debuts. In 1991, I started working with Robert De Niro on **A Bronx Tale** (1993). He hadn't directed, but he certainly had worked with many great directors. He has incredible instincts for story, for cast, and even design and photography. **A Bronx Tale** was a world he knew really well, but he still did a lot of research. We'd spend every weekend listening to every song that came out of that period. He lived that world, he knew those neighborhoods, and he respected those people. He wanted it to be right. It was the same with Ed Harris on **Pollock** (2000), Gary Ross on **Pleasantville** (1998), Tim Robbins on **Dead Man Walking** (1995), and Julian Schnabel on **Basquiat** (1996).

It's a big risk to produce first-time directors' films. Initially, nobody wanted to give Julian Schnabel the time of day. He's a painter. There were a lot of painters at that time who were trying to direct, and most of them who got the chance didn't do a very good job of it. But I recognized that the movie Julian wanted to make was about a world he knew really well. The art world in the 1980s was an arena he knew better than anybody. He knew how to find the truth in the story. I believed in him for that reason. We spent a lot of time together and I saw both his talent as an artist and his love for movies. He is educated in classic world cinema, he has great respect for and rapport with actors and he's a good writer. We put up the seed money ourselves for **Basquiat**. Then we convinced two art collectors to fund the production. Julian basically had to make guarantees that if it didn't pay off, he'd personally get them their money back. We made the movie for $3 million and got it all back. We structured his second film, **Before Night Falls** (2000), the same way. For **The Diving Bell and**

> "If you want to continue to grow and get better at anything, you have to put in the time. Back then, I might have been starting out as a PA, but I was always looking over the shoulder of the DoP or the production designer or the costume designer, and quietly watching the actors and director."

the Butterfly (2007) and **Miral** (2010), we were finally able to get financing. It came from Europe (Pathé). Nobody in the USA was willing to put money in until they saw the finished films. Then we did a documentary with Lou Reed that again was made with private money. Three out of Julian's five films were backed 100 percent by private investors with no distribution or foreign pre-sales. That's real independent filmmaking, and they all made it to the big screen. It's been a great partnership and friendship. I am very proud of the work that's come out of it.

The challenge for me is to make something out of nothing. It's very different when a producer is handed a script and a bunch of money from a studio. I never had that—not by an inability to get it, but by choice. I always felt it would be a little less pure in a way because then you have to serve another master. When I've worked with studios it's usually on a negative pick-up basis, with the studio getting behind the filmmaker's vision. When I'm paying my own bills and working out of my house, I don't have to answer to anybody. I don't have the pressure of some overhead deal that's driving it all. I just want to make the films I want to make with the people I want to make them with, and be able to give the directors the help they need. And, at the same time, find partners—whether they are studios, independents, foreign distributors or private investors—who will back us. I've been able to pull it off so far.

02 **A Bronx Tale** (1993), Robert De Niro's directorial debut

Bill Kong

"I always believe that in the relationship between a producer and a director, you have to be best friends and best partners. How I would define best friends is that when your best friend is in trouble, you would do anything you could to cover him. As best partners, you both share the same vision."

Hero (2002)

Since producing **Crouching Tiger, Hidden Dragon** (2000), Bill Kong has emerged as one of the most influential figures in Asian cinema. A modest and self-deprecating character, he has nonetheless pulled together some of the most ambitious and complicated films ever made in China—projects of the scope of Zhang Yimou's **Hero** (2002) and Ang Lee's **Lust, Caution** (2007)—many of which have a knack for crossing over to western audiences.

Kong studied engineering in Vancouver—an unlikely background for Hong Kong's pre-eminent producer. However, he also comes from a filmmaking family. In 1959, his father Kong Cho Yee founded Edko Film, the first Chinese-run independent film company in Hong Kong, which for more than half a century has been a leading distributor and exhibitor.

Kong co-produced Tian Zhuangzhuang's **The Blue Kite** (1993), one of the key films made by the so-called Fifth Generation of Chinese filmmakers, which fell foul of the censors and was banned in China. Nonetheless, after 1997, when Hong Kong was handed back to the Chinese authorities after 150 years of British rule, Kong again looked to China.

As a distributor, Kong had worked very closely with the directors whose movies he went on to produce, most notably Ang Lee and Zhang Yimou. Alongside films for both these directors and art-house fare like **Springtime in a Small Town** (2002), he has made genre films and has also worked with many younger directors. It is striking that when asked to consider his proudest career achievements, he points to **Ocean Heaven** (2010), about a father's relationship with an autistic son, as readily as he does to the Oscar-winning **Crouching Tiger, Hidden Dragon**.

INTERVIEW

Bill Kong

" My father was a very prominent exhibitor back in the 1960s in Hong Kong and we grew up watching movies in cinemas. My father had also founded Edko Film in 1959, which I subsequently inherited. So I did grow up in a family where we watched movies from a very young age. The two films I have most memory of are **The Guns of Navarone** (1961) and **The Magnificent Seven** (1960). They were films that I watched many times in my father's theaters.

I wouldn't say that I was raised to take over the business. My father was very liberal and never interfered in or directed what we wanted to do —he just let us decide ourselves. So I studied engineering. I have a degree in civil engineering. I discovered my real interest subsequently. I wasn't even sure what I wanted to do when I was in my 20s, you know. I'd say I really knew what I wanted to do when I got to my late 20s and early 30s. So I wouldn't say I was groomed into doing this, not at all.

At that time, when I was deciding what I wanted to do, I was hanging around the offices of my father, as most Chinese kids do. I slowly grew into it. In the beginning, my father asked me to take charge of marketing. Subsequently, I took over the marketing department of the company. Then, my father said, "why don't you go and do acquisitions." From there I merged into the role of buying movies as a distributor. I grew into that step by step. With the early films I marketed, I had a couple of very, very big failures. I was stung by the failures and learned from my mistakes. The most important thing that I remember that gave me confidence and pushed me into this deep passion for movies was, I think, distributing the Miyazaki animation. In the early 1980s, I bought the first few Hayao Miyazaki animations and I turned them into giant hits in Hong Kong. I experimented with using big names to dub the animation. That became very successful. From then on, I had a 12-year relationship with [Miyazaki's company] Studio Ghibli until they merged with Disney.

One of my early plunges into making movies was **The Blue Kite** (1993) and I was mostly a

Working with Zhang Yimou and Ang Lee

(02–03) In his partnerships with Chinese director Zhang Yimou and Taiwanese-born American filmmaker Ang Lee, Kong has discovered two kindred spirits. He was the distributor of their films before he was their producer. He talks with huge respect not just about their artistry, but about their professionalism. They are, as he puts it, "best friends and best partners."

"I knew Ang because when he made his first movie, **Pushing Hands** (1992), I was the distributor of that film for Hong Kong," he observes. "I went onto distribute every single one of his films since then. Our friendship started when he made his first movie. We get along very well. My relationship with him can be described in one word—trust. I trust him with everything I have and vice versa. I never have any doubts about anything he says."

He is equally admiring about Zhang Yimou. "When I am making his movie, honestly I don't even need to be on set. All I need to do is put the thing together and then it will run like clockwork." **(02)** Ang Lee (right) on the set of **Crouching Tiger, Hidden Dragon** (2000). **(03)** Zhang Yimou (left) on the set of **A Woman, a Gun and a Noodle Shop** (2009).

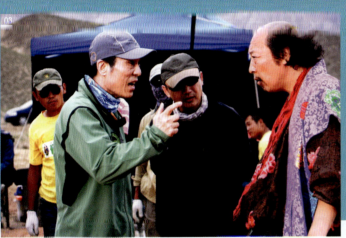

co-producer. I wasn't on the set so much because I was still very busy distributing movies. At that time, China was just opening up and everything was so unknown. I had been into China with my father in the late 1980s. It was very dark and we were just stretching out our hand and feeling our way around. We couldn't see anything. Nobody knew which direction it was going in. The market was very immature and people didn't have money yet. But we knew the potential was there. We knew from day one that this was a place where there was a lot of opportunity in the future. But we were very cautious. Me and my father are very conservative people and so we just went very, very slowly—step by step. We'd buy some movies for China, produce one or two movies, build one or two cinemas. We were not doing it on a very large scale. The Chinese market at that time was very, very closed. Many things weren't really allowed. 1997 was a very important year for Hong Kong. It was the time that Hong Kong went back to China. There was a lot that was unknown and there were many uncertainties in Hong Kong at that time. Because of that uncertainty, the economy was very bad and the film business suffered. I remember that after the film **Titanic** (1997), business was very bad and local production was almost nothing. At the same time, for us independent distributors, buying film was extremely difficult. I remember we had tried to buy **Basic Instinct** (1992) in the early →

> "I don't kid myself that I am going to be looking at success every day. I always feel when you make movies, some are going to be hits and some are going to be misses."

01 Springtime in a Small Town (2002), directed by Tian Zhuangzhuang

> "I find it very inspiring to work with first-time or second-time directors. I spend a lot of time with these young people because I really enjoy working with them."

nineties. We were offering so much money, but we were still outbid by a competitor and that competitor went on and made money. The next year, I went in and offered over $1 million for Hong Kong rights to a film called **Lolita** (1997), but I was still outbid by my competitor. At that time, buying one film like **Lolita** for five years for Hong Kong cost over US $1 million. I thought—I can make two movies for $1 million and I can have the rights forever! Then I realized that spending my time competing with my competitor to buy films was not the future for me. I devolved myself into making movies. That's when I partnered with Ang Lee and made **Crouching Tiger, Hidden Dragon**. I don't recall that I had very much difficulty with that transition from distributor to producer. Even when we were distributors, we were reading a lot of scripts. I remember going to Cannes, I would be reading scripts until three or four in the morning. We're very used to reading two or three scripts a day before we go into the market. For me, changing that into creative work was not difficult.

I began to learn to deal with actors. That was a big challenge for me. That was the experience that I had to learn—and that I am still learning. There is no secret. I think the secret at the end of the day is how you yourself behave. How you treat people will reflect back on how they treat you. If you treat people fairly, people will treat you fairly. They might not treat you fairly on day one. If I ever do have a reputation, I think that reputation was well earned. Day one nobody trusts you. You don't have a credit. But as time goes on, year by year, people watch how you treat people and people pay back how you treat them. If you treat them badly, they treat you badly.

Maybe in America, maybe in other markets, you can behave badly, but in this part of the world, it is more difficult. Our industry is driven by talented directors and by the name actors. We don't have a studio system. We don't have a producer system. It is not driven by money at all. If you look at China right now, there are only three bankable directors. At the end of the day, it's word of mouth or your reputation that attracts people to work for you. There are always people that have a lot more money than you do.

Ang Lee is from Taiwan, but he is more than Taiwanese—I think he's more Chinese than any Chinese. If you look at his work or his life—the way he lives—he is beyond Taiwanese. I knew Ang because when he made his first movie, **Pushing Hands** (1992), I was the distributor of that film for Hong Kong. I went on to distribute every single one of his films since then. Ang always has a very strong idea of what he wants to make. If he has an idea or has a book, I will service him with finding the best people to help him realize that. The original idea has always come from him. He always knew what he wanted to make. I think there were a certain number of Chinese films he wanted to make in his life. It was already in his own mind. What I do is support him, help him, and service him with how to realize that dream.

Although I was born in Hong Kong, I was educated in the West. I studied in Canada, at UBC in Vancouver. I spent ten years going to schools and universities in the West. When I look at →

01 House of Flying Daggers (2004), directed by Zhang Yimou

CROUCHING TIGER, HIDDEN DRAGON

(02–05) When Kong began work on **Crouching Tiger, Hidden Dragon** (2000), the Hong Kong industry was in the doldrums. Kong jokes that he struggled to find technicians "because everybody had become taxi drivers and had changed career."

Putting the budget together was difficult. There were few examples of Chinese-speaking movies becoming international successes. Kong and Ang Lee were determined not to make an English-speaking movie. "In the end, Gareth Wigan, an executive at Sony Pictures, promised he would buy the film from us after we had finished. This provided the leverage to borrow money. Because of his endorsement, we were able to make the movie. Then Good Machine helped us find the rest of the budget. They were also very helpful. The budget was something like $15 million. That was the biggest budget for any Chinese movie at that time. We never had an eye on the American market at all. We always had our eye only on the Chinese market," Kong insists. "If you look at the track record, the highest grossing Chinese-speaking movie in America at that time was a movie that took less than $1 million—so how could we count on this film making any more money than that? Getting Chow Yun-Fat, Michelle Yeoh, and Zhang Ziyi was not really for the western market. The film's success in other countries was a total surprise to us—a total pleasant surprise to us."

HERO

(01–02) Hero (2002) was an immensely complex film, a period piece set in 227 BC and featuring extravagant costumes and martial arts sequences. Nonetheless, Kong knew that his director would have plotted everything out well in advance.

"Zhang Yimou is a fantastic filmmaker. Before he starts shooting frame one, he already knows every single frame he wants to shoot. It is already in his mind. He is one of the most prepared directors. He doesn't need to do so many takes. After three or four, he knows what he has already. He told me that the film studio used to only give him 12,000 feet of raw stock. Imagine, he had to use 12,000 feet to shoot a movie that required 10,000 feet. That means you have to know what you are shooting."

myself, I see that half of my mind is trained with a western mindset. I have totally no cultural differences with these people. Our first collaboration with US partners was **Crouching Tiger, Hidden Dragon**, which was a hit and made so much money. I am sure if the first film had been a disaster, things might have been different. Because we started off with a big bang, everybody worked very well with each other.

I learned a lot from that production and I just went on. I don't kid myself that I am going to be looking at success every day. I always feel when you make movies, some are going to be hits and some are going to be misses. I come from a background as a distributor. When I buy a film to distribute, I have a film opening every two weeks in Hong Kong. With the success of **Crouching Tiger, Hidden Dragon**, yes I felt very happy, but it was, okay, what are we going to do next then? I am not the type of person who wants to lean on a success for a long, long time. I want to look at my career, not one or two movies. I am the kind of person who enjoys the process more than the result. I enjoy the process of making the movie. That a successful movie like **Crouching Tiger, Hidden Dragon** was going to the Oscars was good, but I feel just as happy with a film that is less successful. Two years ago, I made a movie

> "We don't have a studio system. We don't have a producer system. It is not driven by money at all. If you look at China right now, there are only three bankable directors."

called **Ocean Heaven** (2010), which was about autistic people, and I had 100 parents thanking me. They were in tears. I never felt so happy in my life. I was even more happy than going up to receive an Oscar.

I believe my background in distribution, in buying movies in the independent world gave me a tremendous help to put me where I am today. That's why today I always encourage independent distributors to go into production.

I had known Zhang Yimou as early as the years of **The Blue Kite** [on which Zhang was cinematographer]. Again, I have been distributing his movies since the 1990s; that's how we knew each other. That's how we struck up a friendship and a relationship.

I always believe that in the relationship between a producer and a director, you have to be best friends and best partners. How I would define best friends is that when your best friend is in trouble, you would do anything you could to cover him. As best partners, you both share the same vision. I look at both of them—Ang Lee and Zhang Yimou—as best friends and best partners. We always do things together, we share the same vision, and we try to cover each others' backs.

Zhang Yimou is a fantastic filmmaker. He knows exactly what he wants. When I am making his movie, honestly I don't even need to be on set. All I need to do is put the thing together and know that it will run like clockwork. He is like any other director. He is an artist and making movies is his life. He is happiest when he is on set. He is so happy that he doesn't need to sleep. I think as a filmmaker, he just wants to indulge fully in the subject matter. Artistically, he wants to venture into different subjects and different worlds. Even doing the Olympics [Yimou directed the 2008 Beijing Olympics opening ceremony] was something like that, showing off what he can give to the world. He doesn't want to do one specific type of thing. He tries his best to do different things like Chinese people want to try different kinds of foods.

When people like me have to go to The Film Bureau regularly, we have to deal with the officials all the time. We'll know what the climate of this year is. We know what they are looking for and what to avoid. They call us and tell us. We didn't get into such a lot of trouble with **Lust, Caution** (2007). The film was passed and shown in China. For the Chinese version, they took out some sex scenes. It was only after the film finished its run that the controversy erupted. We weren't penalized. Some people on the internet criticized the movie. That's all.

With **The Flowers of War** (2011)—which is set during the Rape of Nanking—there was a lot of speculation and concern when we were making the movie, even from The Film Bureau. 2012 is the 40-year anniversary of the normalization of Sino-Japanese relations. In terms of China, they didn't want to make anything that upset Japan and tried to upset or provoke Chinese people [into hating] the Japanese. A lot of people were very nervous, but if you do see the movie, you see it's not anti-Japan at all. The background is the Nanking massacre, but there's no massacre in the film. It's not about that. It's a story about human beings' triumph—about how brave Christian Bale's character is. He was a nobody, a runaway. It's how a normal human being triumphed through difficulties. →

03 Curse of the Golden Flower (2006). Zhang's epic starring Gong Li

"The two films I have most memory of are **The Guns of Navarone** (1961) and **The Magnificent Seven** (1960). They were films that I watched many times in my father's theaters."

The other films I do are always with new filmmakers. After working with Yimou and Ang, I developed an interest in working with new directors. I find it very inspiring to work with first-time or second-time directors. I find them everywhere. People submit their scripts; people send me their short films. I seldom work with a director who has come with a pitch. I usually encourage them to write a script. They have to use their best efforts at least to write a script. Otherwise, I don't think they are seriously committed to being a director. Combining running Edko with producing, I try not to sleep very much! I have very, very good people working around me. Most of my time I spend on making movies. "

01 Under the Hawthorn Tree (2010)

LUST, CAUTION

(02–03) Taiwan-born director Ang Lee said that he made **Lust, Caution** (2007) primarily for Chinese audiences. However, the film's strong sexual content meant that it was heavily cut before it was shown in mainland China. Back in the West, its laborious engagement with the details of Chinese and Hong Kong politics in the late 1930s and early 1940s was clearly offputting for some audiences. There was also controversy over whether this was a Taiwanese film. It was put up as Taiwan's entry for the Oscars, but the Academy rejected it on the grounds that it had no financing or cast from the island. All the issues underlined the challenges that face a producer working between East and West. **(02)** Ang Lee with cinematographer Rodrigo Prieto on set.

THE FLOWERS OF WAR

(04–06) In the words of Bill Kong, **The Flowers of War** (2011) is "a story about human beings' triumph," a redemptive about people and how the best side of people comes out at the most difficult time. This was an important point to make. Zhang Yimou's film is set during the Rape of Nanking in 1937, when Japanese soldiers overran the Chinese city and committed unspeakable atrocities. Both Kong and the director were determined to emphasize that the film wasn't intended to stoke anti-Japanese feeling or prejudice. **(05)** Zhang with actor Christian Bale on set.

Staying true to your roots

Kong is often asked why he has never produced films in the USA. His response is that he is not qualified. "If I go to America, I've counted that there are two million producers better than I am. But in China, I have an edge. There are not many people better than I am—and why do I want to waste my time competing with two million great producers!"

LEGACY

Dino De Laurentiis

Born in 1919 outside of Naples, Italy, the son of a pasta maker, Agostino "Dino" De Laurentiis rose to become one of the most prolific and innovative international producers of his time. With a career spanning 70 years, he made more than 150 films, won two Oscars, and was an early pioneer of financing films by pre-selling them territory by territory.

As a teen, De Laurentiis left home to study acting in Rome. He quickly became fascinated by what was going on behind the camera and turned his focus to producing. While World War II delayed the start of De Laurentiis' career, he steadily made films from the mid-1940s on. Emerging from the ravages of war, De Laurentiis and his neorealist compatriots were eager to put their "dreams" on screen and their work quickly gained global recognition.

De Laurentiis' 1949 production **Bitter Rice**, starring his wife, actress Silvana Mangano, was nominated for the foreign-language Oscar. Two later films directed by Federico Fellini, **La Strada** (1954) and **Nights of Cabiria** (1957), won Oscars. Both were also produced by Carlo Ponti, with whom De Laurentiis partnered during much of the 1950s.

In that same decade, De Laurentiis began looking to make films with a wider international appeal. He ramped up Tolstoy adaptation **War and Peace** (1956) and hired American director King Vidor and Hollywood stars Audrey Hepburn, Henry Fonda, and Mel Ferrer. It was also one of the first major films De Laurentiis sold territory by territory, versus to one main studio distributor.

The producer took his fondness for lavish epics based on classic books to another level when he turned his focus on biblical tales, most notably with **Barabbas** (1961), starring Anthony Quinn; and later, more literally, with **The Bible** (1966). French director Robert Bresson had been hired for **The Bible**, but when he decided to shoot only animal footprints and not the animals in the Noah's Ark scenes, he was taken off the film. De Laurentiis quickly flew to Mexico to ask

01 De Laurentiis on the **King Kong** (1976)

> "Emerging from the ravages of war, De Laurentiis and his neorealist compatriots were eager to put their 'dreams' on screen and their work quickly gained global recognition."

John Huston—who was shooting **The Night of the Iguana** (1964) at the time—to take over. De Laurentiis had tried to make a deal with Columbia for the film, but when he read their proposed contract, it was so heavily in favor of the studio, the producer famously said to the Paramount executives, "Gentlemen, you forgot one thing…" and dropped his trousers. He self-financed **The Bible** and later made a deal with Twentieth Century Fox to distribute it. The film was shot in part at Dinocitta, the studio complex De Laurentiis had built just outside of Rome. Among his other films to shoot at Dinocitta was Roger Vadim's **Barbarella** (1968), starring Vadim's wife at the time, Jane Fonda.

The producer left Italy for the United States in the 1970s and quickly made his mark. He optioned Peter Maas' novel *Serpico* for $100,000 while it was still being written. He had read the first chapter and was intrigued by the description of the character that would eventually be played by Al Pacino in the 1973 Sidney Lumet film.

De Laurentiis went on to produce films including **Death Wish** (1974), **Three Days of the Condor** (1975), and the 1976 remake of **King Kong**, which gave Jessica Lange her acting debut. He also helped boost Arnold Schwarzenegger's career with **Conan the Barbarian** (1982).

De Laurentiis' choices in material varied wildly. He could move from literary epics to sci-fi to gritty New York stories and action films. He produced Milos Forman's E.L. Doctorow adaptation **Ragtime** (1981), which was nominated for eight Oscars, and also made several films based on Stephen King novels and Thomas Harris' books about serial killer Hannibal Lecter (though not **The Silence of the Lambs**). While he had critical and commercial hits, De Laurentiis also suffered various disappointments over the years with films such as **Orca** (1977), **Flash Gordon** (1980), **Dune** (1984), and **Hannibal Rising** (2007).

In his final years, De Laurentiis worked out of offices on the Universal Studios lot. His bungalow, which decades before had housed Alfred Hitchcock, was neighbored on one side by the studio offices of toymaker Hasbro. A giant Mr. Potato Head fixture, courtesy of Hasbro, loomed nearby. It must have been a less-than-cheerful reminder of how American studio tastes had shifted to "tentpole" movies based on toys and brands. De Laurentiis passed away in 2010.

02 Barbarella (1968), directed by Roger Vadim and starring Jane Fonda

03 The Bible (1966), directed by John Huston

Jon Landau

"Jim and I have worked together for 17 years. That's a long time to work with anybody. Especially in a business that is as intense as the film industry. So you have to find the opportunities where you can just step back. The role of a producer is both to be the Devil on the shoulder and the Angel on the shoulder. You just have to figure out which times to be which."

Avatar (2009)

As the producer of the two highest grossing films of all time, **Titanic** and **Avatar**, Jon Landau keeps a relatively low profile. Landau has been director James Cameron's hands-on producer ever since he was hired to produce **Titanic** (1997), for which they won the Best Picture Academy Award. The two first met when Landau was an executive at Twentieth Century Fox in the early 1990s. Landau currently holds the COO title at Cameron's production company, Lightstorm Entertainment.

Landau grew up around the arts in New York, where his parents Ely and Edie Landau produced independent films (**Long Day's Journey Into Night**, 1962; **The Man in the Glass Booth**, 1975, **Hopscotch**, 1980). He followed into their profession, starting on small films in the 1970s. The work eventually took Landau to Los Angeles, where his first full producing job came on RKO/Paramount's **Campus Man** (1987). Though that film didn't turn heads, Landau was able to move on to bigger studio projects.

The visual effects experience Landau gathered on Disney's **Honey, I Shrunk the Kids** (1989) brought him the opportunity to work as a co-producer on another Disney project, Warren Beatty's comic adaptation **Dick Tracy** (1990). From there, Landau took an executive position as head of physical production at Fox, where he worked on films including **The Last of the Mohicans** (1992), **Power Rangers** (1995), **Mrs. Doubtfire** (1993), **Aliens 3** (1992), and **True Lies** (1994).

He followed his studio stint with **Titanic** and joined Cameron at Lightstorm, where Landau served as a producer on Steven Soderbergh's sci-fi remake **Solaris** (2002) before embarking on the multi-year development journey for **Avatar** (2009). The 3D phenomenon broke new ground with performance-capture technology and techniques. Landau and Cameron were again nominated for the Best Picture Oscar, though **The Hurt Locker** (2008) took the prize in 2010. But Landau and team had plenty to celebrate when the film went on to shatter all-time revenue records, including the one held by their own reigning champ, **Titanic**.

More **Avatar** films are in the works.

INTERVIEW

Jon Landau

"I see a producer's role as all encompassing. I see it from the script, to the financing, to the casting, to the casting of the crew, to the production, to the editing, to the marketing, to the merchandising and beyond. Every movie is a start-up company, and as a producer you are the COO of that company. Your business plan is the script. Other people might hire engineers, you hire production designers. You have to create a product and bring it to the marketplace and sell it in a much shorter period of time than Proctor & Gamble or Mercedes-Benz puts out a new product. That to me is both challenging and exciting.

On **Avatar** (2009), I was out merchandising and marketing the movie quite a bit. We would have a dog-and-pony show where we'd show material. But I was the dog, and the footage was the beautiful pony. I went to probably all but one continent in the world trying to sell them the idea of **Avatar**—the exhibition, the 3D aspects, merchandizing partners, and promotional partners. One of the more exciting things for me about **Avatar** is that it was a movie where you had the opportunity to go and work with a Mattel, or to go and deal with a McDonald's, or to go to Russia and introduce them to 3D movies that they had never even heard of before. And now we're discussing a Disney theme park for **Avatar**. I really enjoy that whole concept and being able to wear many hats as a producer. At the budgetary levels that we've produced our recent movies, we look to the major studios to finance them. But we have to sell the movies into those studios. It's not like the studios think, "Jim Cameron's doing it, it's an obvious thing for us to do." I will always remember what Jim said to me on **Titanic** (1997), when it was touch and go as to whether we were going to get it made: "Jon, it is a producer's responsibility to get a greenlight on a movie." I took that to heart. I took it to heart on **Titanic**, and I took it to heart on **Avatar**.

I think the most important skill for any filmmaker—and I won't limit it to producers—is identifying the objectives of the movie at the beginning and never losing sight of those objectives as you go through the process. Nobody sets out to make a bad movie. Somehow on the journey of making a movie, people go off course. Somebody will say, "Gee we need more action in the movie," and people respond, "Okay, more action!" Some will say, "We need more comedy." "Okay, more comedy!" You get there and you've forgotten it wasn't an action movie and it wasn't a comedy. You can never bring it back. It's about identifying a bull's eye that is very, very far away. As you go down the course of making that film, you're always keeping your eye on it. If you do that, you might not hit the bull's eye, but you'll end up on target. It's the

CAMPUS MAN
(01) Actors Kim Delaney and Steve Lyon in **Campus Man** (1987), Landau's first film as a full-fledged producer. During the shoot, he remembers that producer Barbara Boyle had a bit of wisdom for him. She told Landau: "Jon, nobody ever remembers a bad movie that came in under budget."

> "Every movie is a start-up company, and as a producer you are the COO of that company. Your business plan is the script. Other people might hire engineers, you hire production designers."

responsibility of the producer to keep everybody else's eye on that, too. People tend to become myopic in their own area. As a producer you have to step them out of that and say, "Hey, look at the big picture, this is why we're making the movie and this is our goal in making the movie." I continue to learn things on every film. The learning doesn't stop.

My first job in the business was on a movie-of-the-week called **Found Money** (1983), starring Sid Caesar and Dick van Dyke. Producer Jonathan Bernstein hired me on that film. I'd been working on some very early film-budgeting and scheduling programs for the computer. Jon was fascinated by that, and that was my entrée to being the gopher on the set. I was sort of forced onto the assistant director team, and they of course did not want me on the show because they wanted their own people. They assigned me to take home and charge the walkie-talkies every night, which meant I had to be on the set even before the location department in the morning. They then assigned me to take the film to the lab every evening, which meant I had to stay on the set until the camera crew had wrapped and do that drop off. I loved it. When that little six-week shoot was over, Jonathan asked me to stay on and work in the accounting office. I had no interest in accounting and I had no interest in filing, which was the job they wanted me to do, but I said, "Yes." I learned more over those two weeks of filing than I'd learned on the set. I read everything I filed.

Take whatever opportunity's presented—you never know what you're going to gain. I was offered an opportunity to work as a producer's assistant on a movie called **Beat Street** (1984), which was really a launching point for my career in the film business. A couple of things happened on this film: The gentleman I was working for, line producer Mel Howard, had to take a leave of absence. Although they brought someone else in to replace him, I was the continuity and, all of a sudden, I was stepping up into a larger role on the production. It was a great learning experience. Then, at the end of production,

02 Disney's visual effects-laden **Honey, I Shrunk the Kids** (1989)

Kerry Orent, who was supposed to supervise post-production, wasn't done with **The Cotton Club** (1984), which Francis Ford Coppola had been filming in New York. They asked me to stay on for post-production, so I said, "Yes." They didn't know I knew nothing.

I remember a time when the music supervisor came to me and said we were not going to be able to make our delivery date. We went to relay this to the film's producer, David Picker. David didn't get upset, he just very matter-of-factly looked at both of us and said, "I pay the two of you to tell me how it can get done, not that it can't get done," and he got up and walked out. I will always remember that. Our goal is to figure things out. Later, I was hired by RKO Pictures to make a movie for Paramount called **Campus Man** (1987), on which the director didn't stay on to finish post-production. I got to sort of fill the director's shoes as we finished this movie. Another great learning experience.

Disney then offered me the opportunity to come on as a co-producer on a film called **Teenie Weenies**, which ultimately became **Honey, I Shrunk the Kids** (1989). While I had some exposure to visual effects before that, this film really opened me up to the potential of →

TITANIC

(01–05) One of the crucial aspects of preparing the **Titanic** (1997) shoot was finding the perfect location for the period and action sequences, says Landau. "We'd scouted all around the world on where we could possibly make **Titanic**. One of the things that was important to me, having watched Jim go through **True Lies** (1994), where he was in Washington, DC one day; Providence, Rhode Island the other, and Miami, Los Angeles, Lake Tahoe—that takes its toll on a director creatively. So I wanted to find one location where we could film the entire period part of the movie. We looked at everything; how we were going to do the sinking. We looked at building the ship at the bottom of a rock quarry and filling the quarry with water. We looked at building it in giant blimp hangars, all these different scenarios. But we found this piece of land in Mexico. I had drawn the studio plan on a napkin and that's effectively what we built. It let us do everything in one place—that was the saving grace of the movie. And we did the contemporary footage in Halifax because that's where the Russian research vessel the Keldysh was, which actually went to the wreck of the *Titanic* and we used for the film." **(02–03)** Landau and Cameron on set. **(05)** Landau in Mexico with the ship.

> "I've never had a smooth experience on a film. If you're having a smooth experience on a film, then you are not pushing things far enough. You're not challenging yourself and you're not challenging the others around you."

visual effects. Tom Smith, who was executive producer on the film, had run [visual effects company] ILM before. When we were in post-production, that's when I had the opportunity to meet Warren Beatty and get involved with **Dick Tracy** (1990). Going in to do **Dick Tracy**, all of a sudden I was now the visual effects expert. Because, despite Warren's illustrious career and [cinematographer] Vittorio Storaro's illustrious career, neither one of them had ever really worked in visual effects before.

Following that, I became a studio executive at Twentieth Century Fox to head up and establish their physical production department. I took the studio position with the express purpose of learning how a studio ran from the inside out. I thought we were in a studio-driven business. On the outside, you can't understand all the decisions that go into why a movie is made, why a movie is not made, marketing decisions, etc. I would also join the "weekend read" meetings. To me, you can't separate physical production and creative production. Unless you understand the repercussions of one, you can't make the right decisions in the other, and vice-versa. I would be on location, sometimes for three, four, five months. And after hours, I would do my day job as an executive. I was on location with David Fincher on **Alien 3** (1992), Michael Mann on **The Last of the Mohicans** (1992), and Jim Cameron on **True Lies** (1994)—that's how I got to know Jim.

I was essentially the studio heavy. But the way I approach things in terms of the decision-making process, even as a studio executive, is: It's not the studio's side and the director's side. To me, it's always the movie's side. I'm making this choice not because it's what someone else told me to think or what I think is best for me, it's what's best for the movie. I think those are the decisions that you continually have to make. When I went to **The Last of the Mohicans** set, Michael was having trouble with the schedule and there were some budget questions. One of the first days down there, they were shooting a scene and they weren't going to finish their day. It meant we were going to come back to a location the following Monday. Michael said, "I've figured out a way to shoot this where I don't have to come back on Monday." I said to him, "Michael, don't do that. That'll hurt the scene. We'll come back on Monday, we'll do it the right way and then we'll figure it out." By doing that, Michael knew that anything else that he and I might disagree on down the road, I was still making what I thought was the right decision for the movie.

I was at Fox almost five years. At a certain point, I had to make a decision to leave the studio and go back out and produce on my own. I had a deal in place with Fox to do that. Rae Sanchini, who was president of [James Cameron's company] Lightstorm Entertainment at the time, came to me about a film that they were calling *Planet Ice*, which was the codename for **Titanic**. I read the script and I loved it. It made me cry—it did all those things that you want a script to do. It also spoke to me as a person who likes to make movies. I thought, with the digital evolution, this could be one of the last times where a Hollywood movie is made in the old-fashioned way—where you build the set and have 2,000 extras. That was an exciting thing to realize, and in the middle of it was this incredible love story. I was hired to →

06 *True Lies* (1994). James Cameron with Arnold Schwarzenegger and Jamie Lee Curtis on the set where Landau first worked with the director

"To me, it's always the movie's side. I'm making this choice not because it's what someone else told me to think or what I think is best for me, it's what's best for the movie."

produce the film. One of our first days filming in Halifax, I was on the set and Jim was looking at me and pulled me aside. He said, "Jon, I have a rule. My producers—even if I'm married to them—are only allowed on the set five minutes at a time." He was sort of defining the role. I've tried to show him by example what a producer can do. If you can get a little bit inside the head of a director, you can be their eyes and ears where they can't be. If I was able to go to [production designer] Peter Lamont and say, "Hey Peter, on this set, I think Jim's going to prefer it this way"—because I've remembered it from meetings or that Jim expressed it to me in a conversation—then, when Jim gets to the set, and it is closer to the way he wants it, I've served a function. You can't do that if you're just putting your feet up on a desk in an office. By the time we moved the production to Mexico, Jim kidded that now I had ten minutes on the set. It hasn't really come up since.

Jim and I have worked together for 17 years. That's a long time to work with anybody. Especially in a business that is as intense as the film industry. So you have to find the opportunities where you can just step back. The role of a producer is both to be the Devil on the shoulder and the Angel on the shoulder. You just have to figure out which times to be which.

Every movie is tough in a different way. **Avatar** (2009) was tough in that we were breaking new ground. There were times on **Avatar** where we had to stop to name something. Because if we did not name it, we would never be able to call it back and do it again. On **Titanic**, we had to build a ship, get it to raise and lower, and deal with the outside elements. We tried to do all of our due →

01 Sigourney Weaver and James Cameron on the set of **Avatar** (2009)

AVATAR

(02) "It's our job as a company to make great movies," says Landau. "We look for movies that have a theme that is bigger than their genre. Jim has always done this. If you look at **Aliens** (1986), it is a sci-fi/horror movie, but at the heart of it is a mother-daughter love story. That's why that movie works and that's why Sigourney Weaver gets nominated for an Academy Award. You look at **Avatar**: sure it has the spectacle, but at the heart of **Avatar** are themes that are relatable not just to an American audience, but to a global audience. We live in a global economy today and our movies have to work not just domestically, but internationally."

Pushing boundaries with performance capture

(03–05) From a technologically innovative standpoint, James Cameron's **Avatar** (2009) dazzled in 3D but, more crucially, according to Landau, the film moved the needle on performance capture. "**Avatar** was about the facial performance capture and the virtual production," says the producer. "We said to ourselves, 'If we're going to do this movie, we want Jim to be able to shoot it and work with the cast with the same intimacy that he worked with Kate [Winslet] and Leo [DiCaprio] on **Titanic**.' How do we do that? We can't go to Pandora. So we had to create a virtual Pandora. It was all about Jim and the actors in those moments—and technology that's not all about replacing the actor, but preserving the actor's performance and allowing them to portray characters that they could not otherwise play. So we made the commitment to Sigourney Weaver, to Sam Worthington, to Zoe Saldana, to the rest of our cast, that when they saw those characters in close-up, it would be their performance. That they would be able to recognize their faces." **(04)** Landau with some of the actors during performance capture and **(05)** how this translated to the big screen.

It was also about sharing this new technology with other filmmakers. "One of the great things about Jim is that he does not look at anything that we're doing as proprietary, except for the story. So he's open to share the technology we're employing. The more other people adapt it or adopt it, the more the technology will advance, and the better it will be for us the next time we go to tell a story. What we do is tell stories. If our crew, who we'd taught these skills, goes off and works on **The Adventures of Tintin** (2011) and on **Real Steel** (2011), they will come back to us better prepared," adds Landau, who, along with visual effects supervisor Joe Letteri, shared what they'd learned with Steven Spielberg when he came for a set visit. **(03)** Landau and Cameron on set.

Jon Landau | Interview 123

THE LAST OF THE MOHICANS

(01–03) As head of physical production at Twentieth Century Fox in the early 1990s, Landau spent time on the sets of films such as **The Last of the Mohicans** (1992). **(01)** Director Michael Mann filming on location. **(02)** Landau on location (left) with actor Wes Studi (center).

DICK TRACY

Landau moved on to **Dick Tracy** (1990) after filming **Honey, I Shrunk the Kids** (1989). His director, Warren Beatty, had advice: "Warren said one thing you have to do as a producer is have opinions and you have to be able to articulate the reasoning behind your opinions. Not a lot of people do that. Warren's the type of person who doesn't care where a good idea comes from. So, he was always enlisting people's opinions," says Landau. "He wasn't afraid of them, because he knew, at the end of the day, he was going to make his own decision."
(04) Al Pacino as Big Boy Caprice.

> "I think the most important skill for any filmmaker—and I won't limit it to producers—is identifying the objectives of the movie at the beginning and never losing sight of those objectives as you go through the process."

diligence in picking out the location to film. We had looked at the weather, the precipitation, the light—where the light would fall and how it would cast shadows throughout the ship. We looked at the wind direction: We built the ship into the prevailing winds so that we could blow smoke out of the funnels and it would blow back and make it look like the ship was underway—it would save us a couple of digital-effects shots. The one thing we never thought about checking was fog. We were about to do our big sequence—two weeks on what we called "the tilting poop-deck"—and this fog rolls in. It was there one night, and the next night. We asked the locals about it and they said, "Oh, the fog? It's here from November through February." We thought, Oh my god, we'll never finish this movie! Needless to say, it cleared up and we were able to shoot. We hadn't checked it and there it was, it presented itself to us.

So I've never had a smooth experience on a film. If you're having a smooth experience on a film, then you are not pushing things far enough. You're not challenging yourself and you're not challenging the others around you."

05 Steven Soderbergh's sci-fi remake, **Solaris** (2002)

Andrew Macdonald

 "I would love to be able to write above all else. If you can write a screenplay, that's gold. People don't appreciate that skill enough. As a producer, if you have the material, the doors will open."

Trainspotting (1996)

A maverick producer inspired by US indie filmmakers of the late 1980s and early 1990s, Andrew Macdonald gave British cinema a huge jolt with **Shallow Grave** (1994) and **Trainspotting** (1996). Born in Glasgow in 1966, Macdonald was from filmmaking stock. His grandfather was the mercurial Hungarian screenwriter Emeric Pressburger, who combined with Michael Powell to make such gilt-edged British movie classics as **A Matter of Life and Death** (1946) and **The Red Shoes** (1948). His uncle is James Lee, the boss of Goldcrest during the 1980s.

Macdonald emerged as a producer in Scotland in the mid-1990s. He found important backers in Channel 4 and PolyGram Filmed Entertainment, who were both upping their commitment to film just as his career was starting to blossom. After beginning to collaborate with doctor-turned-writer John Hodge, Macdonald hired Danny Boyle—then best known for TV work like **Mr. Wroe's Virgins** (1993)—to direct **Shallow Grave**. With its style, morbidity and wit, the Edinburgh-set film was as close as British cinema had come to the world of the Coen brothers. It was a minor box-office sensation in the UK. Irvine Welsh adaptation **Trainspotting**, a scabrous tale about heroin addicts in Leith, was even more successful. Both films starred Ewan McGregor.

From these beginnings, Macdonald began to strike outward. His first American film **A Life Less Ordinary** (1997) wasn't as successful as its predecessors; **The Beach** (2000) was notable as Leonardo DiCaprio's first screen outing after **Titanic** had confirmed him as the biggest movie star in the world. **The Beach** made money, but was also mired in controversy.

In 1997, Macdonald and Duncan Kenworthy formed DNA, a new British production company buttressed by around $46 million of national lottery funding. By now, the Macdonald/Hodge/Boyle axis had begun to slip apart. Macdonald was working with other filmmakers. After rocky beginnings and an eventual break with Kenworthy, DNA produced and co-produced some extraordinary films, among them **28 Days Later** (2002), **The Last King of Scotland** (2006) (directed by Andrew's younger brother, Kevin Macdonald), **The History Boys** (2006), and **Notes on a Scandal** (2006).

INTERVIEW

Andrew Macdonald

" I think it's important that as a producer you want to be a director on some level. You want to create; you want to make it happen. There are a lot of producers who are just dealmakers and certain types of facilitators (financiers or whatever). Others are more administrators of all these people and situations. A lot of producers I know—Stephen Woolley, Jeremy Thomas—have directed. I don't think I ever will. But that desire to direct means you want to make a film, you want to be a filmmaker. Everybody who is really involved and offers something to the collaboration is part of the filmmaking team. As a type of producer who wants to make the films, you have to have a wish to see them come to life. I definitely would count myself as one of those producers—a filmmaking producer. As a producer, you have to have a total belief in what you are doing because it takes so long to make a film.

I had directed a short film called **Doctor Reitzer's Fragment** (1991). My brother [Kevin Macdonald] wrote it. It was basically this idea that a film archivist had found this bit of lost film from a film that had been banned for whatever reason. After I had made that short film, a 25-minute film, I decided I was not going to be a director. I was going to be a producer. Even making a short film, most of it was about organizing everything, calling in favors.

I wanted to find a piece of material to produce. I met [the writer] John Hodge through his sister. She was working as an assistant editor at a place called The Film Editors, which was Ridley Scott's commercials company. I figured that Scotland was a much better place to start. It was a smaller place. It was where I came from. I had been working there and I knew all the crew. Scotland then in the early 1990s was going through a creative boom. Glasgow was in particular, with the "year of culture" in 1990. Having been in America, I was also really interested in the American independent cinema with its "can do" attitude, particularly the Coens and Spike Lee. They had made these films with private money. No one was making films with private money at the time. I felt most British cinema at the time was dull beyond belief.

I was about 25 or 26 years old when I met John Hodge, who was a doctor. He wanted to write a screenplay or to be a playwright. He had written this idea—which became **Shallow Grave**

SHALLOW GRAVE

(01–02) Macdonald went to Edinburgh to shoot **Shallow Grave** (1994), his first attempt to make a low-budget, independent British film that had the attitude and ingenuity of the US indie films he so admired. "They [the US directors] were making films with a lot of integrity that were also accessible." The project marked the first collaboration between Macdonald, director Danny Boyle, and writer John Hodge. Boyle had recently enjoyed success as a director with **Mr. Wroe's Virgins** (1993), made for the BBC, but was determined to make a big-screen movie. With the patronage of David Aukin at Channel 4 and the marketing wizardry of PolyGram Filmed Entertainment to boost it, **Shallow Grave** turned into a substantial British success.

01

> "I think it's important that as a producer you want to be a director on some level. You want to create; you want to make it happen."

(1994)—about people sharing a house and the [dead] body. Also, he had this wonderful tone of writing, this black comedy. We spent a bit of time discussing the script and working on it, him doing the writing and me making suggestions. My suggestions were a lot about how we were going to make this an American way for an American price. We moved the story to a flat. I was obsessed with American independent cinema at that time—**She's Gotta Have It** (1986), **Blood Simple** (1984), **Sex, Lies, and Videotape** (1989) and all that. They [the indie US filmmakers] were making films that had a lot of integrity, but were also accessible.

I had a relationship with the Scottish Film Board and they gave us a little money to develop **Shallow Grave**. Through that, we met businessman and screenwriter Allan Scott [the alias of Allan Shiach]. He became our champion. He gave us a little office in his building in London. We had a script that people were beginning to quite like. I gave it to the newly appointed head of film at Channel 4, David Aukin. I remember him ringing me up in my flat one day and saying "do you want to make a film together."

I met a few directors. Danny Boyle was one →

04 Macdonald on the set of **Shallow Grave**

03 Danny Boyle (left) with John Hodge (center) and Andrew Macdonald (right) promoting **Shallow Grave** in Dublin

> "I remember David Puttnam telling me, 'you're an idiot to make the film because no one will watch it.' Something I might say to a younger producer now who wanted to make a film set in the world of heroin addiction."

of the ones who wanted to do it. He was just like he is now. He was extremely enthusiastic and dying to make a feature film. He got it in terms of the tone and he wasn't scared of the black humor or the violence that we were pushing. Instantly, he started to make the film better creatively. He had been passed over for other films. That was to my advantage. He immediately saw it as an opportunity and a way to form a relationship that could be useful to him. That led to the partnership between the three of us—a very loose thing. I had control over the very limited amount of net profits Channel 4 gave us for our first film and I decided we would split all.

Shallow Grave was very, very successful. It made $8 million at the UK box office, which I'd still be pleased with today. It also made $8 million in France. PolyGram bought the film when it was finished. They were prepared to take quality films that were accessible and spend a lot of money marketing them. We went quickly into **Trainspotting** with the same partners. I wanted to make it for a low price and get on with it because it was very difficult material. A friend of mine had given me the book. First of all I needed to convince Danny and then John, who had to write it. It wasn't that hard to convince Irvine Welsh [the novelist], but there were a lot of people around Irvine. It was Irvine's first book and he had signed over everything, including film rights to this company, and they were pretty tricky. That was my first little lesson—making films is just one continual process of lawyers and management. Irvine himself was an incredibly generous, easygoing guy who has since collaborated with many different filmmakers.

Trainspotting was a dream project. We hit that "Cool Britannia" moment, but there was no intention to do that. We were just that age and made that film. It all seemed very natural. When we started doing the book, we were doing it for the right reasons. I remember David Puttnam telling me "you're an idiot to make the film because no one will watch it." Something I might

04 Danny Boyle (far right) on the set of Trainspotting with Andrew Macdonald (left) and John Hodge (center)

TRAINSPOTTING

(01–02) A scabrous tale about drug addicts in Leith, Macdonald's adaptation of Irvine Welsh's *Trainspotting* didn't seem an obvious candidate for box-office success. However, the film, released in 1996, was made with a riotous energy that chimed perfectly with the mood of the times. This was the era of "Cool Britannia." Macdonald recruited bands like Leftfield and Primal Scream to give the film credibility. PolyGram marketed it as if it was a wild new rock album, plastering posters on bus shelters and billboards all over Britain. The British launch was followed by a huge and very decadent party at the Cannes Festival. "We knew we had something pretty good because it [Trainspotting] had been a success in the UK, and what we tried to do was flaunt that and create as much of a stir as possible. PolyGram had this private jet. We used it almost like a bus. We invited our own people and got them flown up and down," Macdonald recalled of the party where the guests ranged from venerable US director Robert Altman to British rock star Noel Gallagher.

> "**Trainspotting** was a dream project. We hit that 'Cool Britannia' moment, but there was no intention to do that. We were just that age and made that film."

say to a younger producer now who wanted to make a film set in the world of heroin addiction.

Those two films—**Shallow Grave** and **Trainspotting**—were shot in six or seven weeks. They were edited in six and seven weeks. They were cut on film. They were previewed and they were considered good. There were little changes.

The Weinsteins [at Miramax] were excited about the idea of being in business with Danny and had pre-bought the film. That was a great deal for Channel 4 because it gave them no risk. We felt creatively we were in a very strong place. I had decided that a relationship with an American studio was the right next step and that Fox with Fox Searchlight was a good place to work with. We built some good relations there with Tom Rothman and Peter Rice. Those relationships continue today.

With **A Life Less Ordinary** (1997), we were trying to make a film in America, but under our terms. We messed up creatively on that film. Originally, the film was about a Scottish guy →

03 From left to right: Ewan McGregor, Macdonald, Danny Boyle, Irvine Welsh, and John Hodge

THE BEACH

(01) Making a big-budget studio film in Thailand with the world's then biggest movie star was always going to be a challenge. Macdonald is full of praise for lead actor Leonardo DiCaprio—"he loves films, he knows exactly what he wants to do"—but acknowledges that shooting **The Beach** (2000) was very tough. The process wasn't made any easier when he ended up caught in the crossfire as an international controversy broke out over the alleged damage the filmmakers were doing to the environment. In spite of all the teething pains and problems, the film was still a substantial international success at the box office.

Working with studios: the Faustian pact

You have to find a balance when you work with studios. As Macdonald points out, "the great thing about studios is that they are distributors—the best distributors in the world. If you make films for them that they like, you are much more successful. They'll finance them. They'll release them quickly. You'll get a nice statement that will say they've released the film in 60 territories. It's all about making money. The downside is that the studios have a limited capacity. A narrower band of what creatively they want and you lose control both day-to-day and of your ownership. They become the producer."

SUNSHINE

(02–03) Sunshine (2007), shot at 3 Mills Studios in London, saw Macdonald, director Danny Boyle and writer Alex Garland venturing into the world of Stanley Kubrick-style sci-fi. The film, about eight astronauts traveling deep into space to try to reignite the dying sun, was made under a joint venture Macdonald's company DNA had set up with US studio, Fox. With a $36-million budget and extensive special effects, this was a hugely ambitious endeavor for an independent British producer. Macdonald was able to make the film partly because of the lottery franchise he and fellow producer Duncan Kenworthy had won in 1997, when they jointly formed DNA. Although Kenworthy subsequently left the company and the initial performance of DNA was patchy, the $46 million in UK lottery public funding was vital in securing the company's long-term future. Without it, DNA would not have been able to strike the deal with Fox or make a film as big as Sunshine. The History Boys (2006), Notes on a Scandal (2006), and The Last King of Scotland (2006) were all also backed by Fox/DNA.

> "**The Beach** was the first time we had done a film 100% owned by a studio and so it added many complications. Everybody had an opinion."

> "The future of independent film is looking difficult, not because of the stories or talent, but the rules of distribution are changing. It feels like television is where we'll end up."

and a French girl. That's the way we should have done it, with a Scottish guy taking a French girl from Paris to Scotland and the mountains.

You learn a whole list of things—how to deal with Hollywood agents and managers and all that stuff. The main thing I learned very early on was that I tried to own the material and to partner with the writer and the director, and then take the package to the market. I think development deals, first-look deals and overhead deals are very difficult things to make work. As a producer, you have to be the owner and the businessman. When you do your first deal with the studio, you get all these documents—the contracts and so forth. The contract says, "the producer shall do this" and "the producer shall do that." You think, oh right, the producer has a lot of rights. Then you realize that they [the studio] are the producer. They're paying for everything and they see themselves as the producer. Producers in Hollywood don't make deals with cameramen, they don't make deals with talent. The studio does all that. It is a completely different way of doing things from being an independent producer, when you do everything yourself and you are in control.

The Beach (2000) was the next film I produced—it was much bigger. I had so much

01 **28 Weeks Later** (2007), directed by Juan Carlos Fresnadillo and starring Robert Carlyle

02 **28 Days Later** (2002), directed by Danny Boyle and starring Cillian Murphy

less day-to-day control. This was the first full studio Fox film I had done. They owned **The Beach**. I owned **A Life Less Ordinary**. This one they owned and we were well paid. We brought them the script and Leonardo DiCaprio. Then they made the deals. Leonardo had liked **Trainspotting**. I got to know him a little and Danny had too. Leonardo DiCaprio was no problem on any level. He loves films and has actual ideas about who he wants to work with. He knows exactly what he wants to do.

The Beach was the first time we had done a film 100% owned by a studio and so it added many complications. Everybody had an opinion because Leonardo was the biggest star in the world. In the end, the studio wanted a Danny Boyle/Leonardo DiCaprio film, but we couldn't quite make all that work. I had probably the worst experience. I was in court, caught up in a whole environmental scandal. I felt very, very unhappy with the British press. I remember people like Channel 4 news coming out, not even wanting to interview or find the truth. We were accused of causing environmental damage in a National Park. [As the producer] you were involved in Thai politics and you were involved in American studio politics. What I should have been doing was concentrating on trying to help everybody make a better film. It [**The Beach**] made Fox money. It made us money. The film was very critically panned. That was very difficult, particularly for Danny.

In terms of the stages of producing, I had made two low-budget films that had been incredibly successful. The second one had been massively successful. We could make the films we wanted and various people wanted to work with you. We were generating material. Danny found the novel *The Beach*. We made **A Life Less Ordinary** and a 30-minute film called **Alien Love Triangle** (1999).

At that time, I felt I had done just about everything I set out to do. I started having a family and buying a house, and all that sort of stuff. Your perspective changes slightly. I could have gone to America at that point. It was the →

Audience and education

For Macdonald, one of the producer's most important tasks is to remind all his collaborators of the audience the film is being made for. "Somebody said that the producer is there to remind the writer, the director, and the actors that there is an audience," Macdonald states. "There is a certain amount of truth in that. The producer really is the person or group of people who are the glue that holds it together. You have the audience, the distributor, the creative people—the writer, director, the actors—and the finance."

His advice for would-be producers is to steep themselves in movies. "If someone wants to be a producer, I always say 'watch as many films as you can.' If you don't know your stuff, forget it. Make as many short films and be involved in the making of films as much as you can. Try to find some like-minded collaborators. You're never going to start with Scorsese and Spielberg. You'll have to find your equivalents."

NEVER LET ME GO

(01–03) Like many producers, Macdonald flags up the primacy of the script. It's the foundation on which any decent movie will be built. With Kazuo Ishiguro adaptation **Never Let Me Go** (2010), Macdonald suggests that Alex Garland's screenplay immediately attracted a top-notch young British cast led by Keira Knightley, Carey Mulligan, and Andrew Garfield **(01)**. **(02)** From left to right: Screenwriter Alex Garland, novelist Kazuo Ishiguro, Macdonald, and producer Allon Reich on set.

biggest boom in cinema spending, all the studios were opening specialty departments. Then, this lottery money came along to encourage people to finance new companies. I partnered with [producer] Duncan Kenworthy [in setting up DNA] to access this funding. We were two of the more successful British producers; we had finance and an amazing distribution agreement with PolyGram. Duncan was producing **Notting Hill** (1999) and I was doing **The Beach**—two really huge films. We had created DNA through which we could make films like **Four Weddings and a Funeral** and **Shallow Grave** with PolyGram. But it never took off: PolyGram was sold, and DNA was not a success in the beginning.

Eventually, I realized that what I wanted to do and what Duncan wanted to do were different things, so we separated, and I took the company on and he left. I made this deal with Fox Searchlight. It was a joint venture. I put up £25 million through the lottery funding and Fox put up $25 million to make British films. Eventually we made **28 Days Later** (2002) and **28 Weeks Later** (2007), **The Last King of Scotland** (2006), **The History Boys** (2006), **Notes on a Scandal** (2006),

04 A Life Less Ordinary (1997), starring Cameron Diaz and Ewan McGregor

> "Leonardo DiCaprio was no problem on any level. He loves films and has certain directors he wants to work with. He knows exactly what he wants to do."

Sunshine (2007), and **Never Let Me Go** (2010). We got the creative, the financing, and the distribution right. DNA was and is a very successful company. The future of independent film is looking difficult, not because of the stories or talent, but the rules of distribution are changing. It feels like television is where we'll end up.

My opinion is to think this is how we can get this made and actually sell it. That's what I try to do, helping the writer and director. I wish I could write. I would love to be able to write above all else. If you can write a screenplay, that's gold. People don't appreciate that skill enough. As a producer, if you have the material, the doors will open. In the film business, there are always films that turn out a little bit better or worse than you expect and you have to be able to ride the two out. Not every film can be a success. It's about having a career.

05 Notes on a Scandal (2006), starring Cate Blanchett and Judi Dench

06 The Last King of Scotland (2006)

05

04

06

Edward R. Pressman

"When it comes to choosing which films to make, my motivation can be very director-driven. I take a vicarious creative pleasure in working with a director, so it's really through that collaboration that I'm drawn to a project. It's psychic eroticism or something like that."

The Crow (1994)

Getting his start producing films with American director Paul Williams in the UK, Edward R. Pressman set the tone for his filmmaker-driven, globally-minded independent film career. With more than 80 titles to his credit now, Pressman continues to make films with an indie edge, while also keeping his eye on opportunities in foreign markets.

Pressman established a New York-based production hub with Williams in the late 1960s and bankrolled their first productions with support from his family's toy business. After Williams decided to stop making films, Pressman continued to produce. Over the years, he has helped launch the careers of an eclectic range of directors. The maverick producer made early films by Brian De Palma, Terrence Malick, Oliver Stone, Kathryn Bigelow, Alex Proyas, and crossover talents such as musician David Byrne (**True Stories**, 1986), among others.

Pressman has had ongoing collaborations with many, particularly with Stone: He produced Stone's feature debut, horror-thriller **The Hand** (1981), followed by **Wall Street** (1987), **Talk Radio** (1988), and sequel **Wall Street: Money Never Sleeps** (2010). Pressman and Stone have worked together as producers on multiple films, such as Bigelow's **Blue Steel** (1989) and Barbet Schroeder's **Reversal of Fortune** (1990). Stone also co-wrote **Conan the Barbarian** (1982), which he developed with the producer. Pressman has also collaborated many times with Abel Ferrara, starting with his cult film **Bad Lieutenant** (1992).

Pressman and Malick continue to make films together through their Sunflower Productions label. So far, Sunflower has yielded five projects marked by evocative imagery and global talent and subjects: Ethiopian runner Haile Gebrselassie biopic **Endurance** (1999), Zhang Yimou's comedy **Happy Times** (2000), Hans Petter Moland's Vietnam GI child drama **The Beautiful Country** (2004), David Gordon Green's thriller **Undertow** (2004), and Michael Apted's transatlantic slave trade period drama **Amazing Grace** (2006). Pressman's eponymous production label continues to churn out filmmaker-driven projects spanning various genres. And the producer is also making the most out of his prior successes with new films and television series inspired by iconic films from the Pressman library.

INTERVIEW

Edward R. Pressman

"I grew up around film in New York. My uncle, Moe Lane, owned three movie theaters in the city—two of them up in Washington Heights. I used to sell popcorn there and would watch two double features a day. I loved movies. In high school, I had a teacher who taught modern European history through film. We watched **Triumph of the Will** (1935), **The Blue Angel** (1930), **The Last Laugh** (1924) and the like, which made a great impression. When I was in college, I had a friend, John Ostriker, at Harvard, who introduced me to the Brattle Theatre, where I discovered Bergman, Truffaut, Kurosawa, Godard, and Buñuel. Though I was very interested in film, it seemed totally remote and not something I could pursue because I was always supposed to go into my family's toy business.

I majored in Philosophy at Stanford, and then went to graduate school at the London School of Economics. I took philosophy, political science, and economics—the PPE Program. That's when I met Paul Williams, who was a graduate student at Cambridge. Paul was a very confident guy who had directed some short films at Harvard. We met at a Thanksgiving dinner in London. We talked all night. I had a non-paying job at Columbia Pictures—they called it an attaché back then, now it would be called an intern. Because I was working at Columbia and Paul had done some film work, I thought he was like Cecil B. DeMille and to him I was like Louis B. Mayer.

We formed a partnership almost immediately, a company called Pressman-Williams. We first made a short film at Cambridge, **Girl**, based on The Beatles' song of the same name. We then made three features together: **Out of It** (1969), one of Jon Voight's first films; **The Revolutionary** (1970), with Voight, Robert Duvall, and Seymour Cassel; and **Dealing: Or the Berkeley-to-Boston Forty-Brick Lost-Bag Blues** (1972), which was based on a book by Michael Crichton and his brother Douglas. Then Paul went on a spiritual journey and left the film business—you know, it was the early 1970s. I continued to produce. It was really through Paul that I got into film and gained the confidence to be a producer.

01 Pressman (center) with Seymour Cassel (left) and Jon Voight (right) in London on the set of **The Revolutionary** in 1969

02 Pressman (bottom) with director Paul Williams in the Pressman-Williams office in New York City, circa 1968

CONAN THE BARBARIAN

(03) "Conan the Barbarian (1982) was a tough film to get made because it was a new genre," says Pressman of the long-gestating, graphic novel-based project. "Sword-and-sorcery didn't exist. People thought of the old Steve Reeves sword-and-sandals' movies. In retrospect, it seems like an obvious commercial venture, but it took many years to get that going. I met Arnold through my friend [filmmaker] George Butler. George was making a documentary called **Pumping Iron** (1977) and asked if we'd look at the editing and give comments. I saw this very impressive personality in the film, and I said, 'Who's that?' And it was Arnold, of course. I wondered where he could be cast. I was there with a friend named Ed Summer, who owned the Supersnipe Gallery, a comic bookstore that was backed by George Lucas on New York's East Side. Ed said, 'Conan, of course!' I said, 'What's Conan?' So he took me to his gallery and showed me the paintings by Frank Frazetta on the covers of the Conan books. They looked like Arnold. So it all fit together. It took five years to get the rights. Arnold had an Austrian accent, so no one—including Dino De Laurentiis, who was our partner on the film—wanted Arnold at first, but that was our condition. When I met Arnold, he was very charismatic. He had a star quality before he became a movie star. **Conan** is also how I met Oliver Stone. Oliver was an unknown writer and we were looking for a screenwriter. He showed me a script called **Platoon**, which was amazing. He wrote the first draft of **Conan** and it was like Dante's Inferno; it was an incredible script, but too expensive to make. Oliver and I then went looking for a director and ultimately chose John Milius, with whom Oliver collaborated on the script."

The Pressman-Williams office in New York was adjacent to my family's toy company. The toy company gave me the free credit for the laboratories and the equipment to make our first films, which were done very inexpensively. Our office was like a center of independent film: Brian De Palma, Martin Scorsese and other young filmmakers, along with Paul, hung out there. Making independent films was sort of an anomaly at that time. They were very difficult to get made because there was no institutional source for it; there weren't even any film schools back then. It was all done like a Broadway show, raising money in little bits. **Out of It** was made for about $200,000. By 1969, it was actually finished and picked up by David Picker at United Artists. Though common today, a negative pick-up like that was unheard of at the time. Almost all films then were made in conjunction with the studios or they weren't made at all.

The 1970s were an exciting time in film: Other than Scorsese and De Palma, Steven Spielberg, John Milius, and George Lucas were filmmakers who were just getting started at the time. We got to know Brian, who was a real ringleader. He had completed his two earliest films, **Greetings** (1968) and **Hi, Mom!** (1970). Then he got a break with a studio film, **Get to Know Your Rabbit** (1972), which turned out to be a failure. During that time Brian made a deal with [producer] Ray Stark →

> "I grew up during the period of the auteur theory, and the French New Wave, and the idea of the director and the producer being aligned was the way I've always looked at it. It was us against the world, not in opposition."

for two big studio films, **Sisters** and **Phantom of the Paradise**, but he and Ray had a falling out. While we were making **Dealing** with Paul Williams, Brian called and asked, "Can you get me out of this? Can you buy out Ray Stark and get **Phantom of the Paradise** (1974) and **Sisters** (1973), so we can do them together?" So we did, and we made both of those films.

Another emerging young filmmaker at the time was Terrence Malick. Paul had gone to Harvard and was friendly with writer Jake Brackman, who was close to Terry, so that's how Terry and I met. Terry was in the first class of AFI and had made a film there. So right after **Sisters** we did **Badlands** (1973) with Terry. **Badlands** was financed independently, as well. Max Palevsky, who was a philanthropist, investor, and a great benefactor of Terry's for many years, helped significantly. He was also a major supporter of George McGovern and helped fund *Rolling Stone* magazine and Intel. I think Max invested $50,000 in **Badlands**, but the whole film cost under $300,000, so that was a sizeable contribution. We gathered the rest from family and friends. My mother was very supportive. My father died when I was 16, so I helped my mother run the toy company, and in exchange, the company helped my movie career. I remember during the making of **Badlands**, the line producer got into an argument with Terry; he returned to New York and told my mom, "Don't support this thing, it's a mess, the worst disorganized kind of movie." But she stood by it. She kept helping us.

At that time, I think the French New Wave influenced us all, and film—as well as music— was something that we thought could change the world. We were living in a very political climate. Film critics were really taken quite seriously, and the French Cinémathèque was a major influence. Film seemed to subsume everything. I think I went into it for the same reason I majored in philosophy. It felt like an encompassing field of endeavor. Being involved in making films excited me, and it still does. It's still fulfilling. Each film we make is a bit of a miracle. →

01 **Sisters** (1973) directed by Brian De Palma

02 **Out of It** (1968). Test shots of Jon Voight and Lada Edmund Jr. on location in Atlantic Beach, Long Island, New York

WALL STREET

(03–05) Pressman met filmmaker Oliver Stone while developing **Conan the Barbarian** (1982), which Stone co-wrote. The duo went on to make the seminal film **(03) Wall Street** (1987) and its sequel **(04) Wall Street: Money Never Sleeps** (2010). But the idea for **Wall Street** grew out of Stone's desire to make a film about the 1950s American quiz show scandals. (That subject eventually made it to celluloid in Robert Redford's 1994 film **Quiz Show**.)

"We started working with [screenwriter] Stanley Weiser, who had gone to NYU with Oliver," remembers Pressman of the **Wall Street** evolution. "We talked about the quiz show scandal subject and worked on it for a few months. At one point, Oliver, Stanley, my wife Annie, and I went to a Chilean restaurant in downtown Los Angeles and Oliver declared we shouldn't do a movie about the quiz shows, but about Wall Street—the original title was **Greed**. His father was a broker, my stepfather was a stockbroker, so we both had a familiarity with that world through our fathers. It was a quick shift. We financed the screenplay, and it was very simple: At that time, Oliver was hot as can be—coming off **Salvador** and **Platoon** (both 1986). It was a contest between Warner Bros. and Fox. Both studios wanted it and Fox got it. Scott Rudin was running Fox at the time. The studio had first wanted Warren Beatty for the lead, who was a much bigger star than Michael Douglas at the time. [Douglas' **Fatal Attraction** (1987) hadn't been released yet.] Oliver wanted Michael for the lead; he really stood his ground and got his way. **Wall Street** was not an expensive movie at $16 million, which for a studio film was relatively small. It was the same year as **Broadcast News**; that was Fox's big film and I remember there was real competition for attention. It was very gratifying when we got the Oscar [for Michael Douglas] and **Broadcast News** didn't, because Fox was putting a lot more money behind that film." **(05)** Pressman and Stone on the set of **Wall Street** in New York City in 1987.

Securing the right talent

(01–02) In the early 2000s, Pressman co-founded ContentFilm to make a series of lower-budgeted digital films with the goal of plugging these into the still-developing digital distribution pipelines. Among the most well-known projects to come out of that venture was Jason Reitman's adaptation of Christopher Buckley's novel *Thank You for Smoking*. "I'd seen Jason Reitman's short film and I knew Chris Buckley's book," Pressman says of how he became involved in **Thank You for Smoking** (2005). "Jason was developing it with David Sacks, who was a partner in PayPal. They had gotten to a point where Jason had written a script without owning the rights to the book. When I was involved in ContentFilm, a friend of mine introduced me to David Sacks, who told us he was working with Jason Reitman on this book. So it was very easy to say we'd like to be your partners. Content put up part of the money and David Sacks and his friends put up part of the money, and that's how we financed the film. The key thing to getting that film to coagulate was getting Robert Duvall **(02)**, who we had worked with before. Once he agreed to do it, then everyone else came on board. Aaron Eckhart and all the other cast wanted to work with Duvall. He gave it a stamp of seriousness and substance. So I think that was the key contribution we made, besides putting up some money. With **(01) The Cooler** (2003) it was the same thing. It was very tough to get Bill Macy to agree, and when he did then Alec Baldwin came in. It sometimes takes a certain type of talent—an actor who other actors want to work with."

Nowadays, getting independent films made is easier, but there is the new challenge of getting them marketed because there's such competition. The whole landscape is changing in terms of marketing now; for independent films there is the opportunity and the challenge of using the internet. It depends on the movie's distribution model as to what control you have over the marketing and how you handle it. The film **Bad Lieutenant: Port of Call—New Orleans** (2009) came together relatively quickly with financing from (producer/distributor) Avi Lerner, but the marketing was a different challenge. We pushed hard for certain marketing elements. The film had stellar reviews from critics, but didn't find an audience theatrically. With **The Crow** (1994), we did our own marketing campaign, then gave it to Miramax and provided the marketing money to execute it. A third party put up the funding so we could put the campaign together in our own organization. We worked with a company called Interlink, which did a great job. In the old days, it was affordable to create and market films independently. **Phantom**

> "As an independent company, we're always looking for new ways of finding financing that works within the same creative parameters. That's always part of the game, to try to find new ways to get films made."

of the Paradise was released by Fox and **Badlands** by Warner Bros.; both were failures when they opened. At that time, with a very modest amount of money, one was able to design a campaign and buy television time in a local market. So we were able to re-release both **Badlands** and **Phantom of the Paradise** ourselves. First we went to a small market, Little Rock, Arkansas, and proved it there; then to Memphis, then Dallas, and we proved it in each of these places. The studios were impressed and gained the confidence to re-release the films and take over the marketing. It really established the films' reputation and commerciality. You could be a very important film in Little Rock for something like $15,000 of television time. The same amount of TV time would be much too expensive now, but the internet gives a similar opportunity in a whole new way that's very interesting to me. Some of the projects we're working on lend themselves to this new kind of marketing. This idea of proving films in individual cities using social media marketing is similar to what Paramount did with **Paranormal Activity**, which went on to huge commercial success.

In the 1970s and 1980s, the studios were less bureaucratic. It was very one-on-one; you talked to an individual who could make a decision quickly. At Columbia Pictures, it was David Begelman; at United Artists, David Picker; and at Warners, it was John Calley, with whom we dealt on **Badlands**. During those freewheeling times, studio heads would make deals and decisions quickly. They also made great movies. Both **Taxi Driver** (1976) and **Close Encounters of the Third Kind** (1977) were movies Begelman made for Columbia. Unfortunately, with this freedom came some corruption, as well. [The book *Indecent Exposure*, which Pressman has the rights to, is about Begelman's embezzlement of funds from Columbia Pictures.] Today, you couldn't get away with that, it's so bureaucratized. So, the corruption was the flip side of the coin of being able to make swift decisions—there was a lot of payback and good guys back then, and now it's a lot more corporatized.

03 **Badlands** (1973), directed by Terrence Malick and starring Martin Sheen and Sissy Spacek

When it comes to choosing which films to make, my motivation can be very director-driven. I take a vicarious creative pleasure in working with a director, so it's really through that collaboration that I'm drawn to a project. It's psychic eroticism or something like that. It can be characterized in a very bold way by a filmmaker like Oliver Stone, David Mamet, Kathryn Bigelow or Barbet Schroeder, or in a more quiet way like David Byrne, the Taviani Brothers or Mary Harron. In each case they have a kind of charisma that gets the people around them excited about their vision so it's not just another job. The character of the individual is really expressed in films they make. This charismatic energy galvanizes people around these directors. It can be as wild as Abel Ferrara and Alex Cox or as logical as Terry Malick. It's hard to define it or make it systematic. It's that energy that has really been the impulse for most of the films I've made.

Though most of my films have been director-driven or writer/director-driven, there are some cases where we started with a writer. **Conan** →

Film and family

(01–02) Pressman made **Good Morning, Babylon** (1987)—about Italian brothers who emigrate to America and end up fighting on opposite sides during World War I—with the Italian filmmaker siblings Paolo and Vittorio Taviani. "The Tavianis created a communal feeling; they have the same people work on all their movies and the feeling around that film was very familial," says Pressman, pictured with the Tavianis (center) and fellow producer Giuliani G. De Negri (right) **(01)**.

the **Barbarian** (1982) began with the graphic novel and Oliver Stone's idea to adapt it. Together we went to [director] John Milius. With **Plenty** (1985), the partner was [playwright] David Hare. David and I looked for the director to realize his play cinematically. He wanted a real American director, not a British director. Then we decided on Australian Fred Schepisi. I said, "I thought we wanted an American director," and David said, "The Aussies are more American than Americans."

We also had a great working relationship with the Public Theater, which was a great joy because [founder] Joe Papp was in his prime. We had an understanding that anything that came from the Public Theater, we'd have first shot at—**The Pirates of Penzance** (1983), **Plenty**, **Talk Radio** (1988) all came from the Public. Working in a climate of the theater was quite different from film. At least within the Public Theater community, there was a great communal spirit. People felt they could suggest things that might be considered silly, and weren't self-conscious about it. It was a very different

> "Credits are very odd things in this business. The producer credit today has become so diffuse. Some films have a dozen or more producers on it. I think producers had a higher regard in the traditional studio system."

atmosphere. The film world is a little touchier; working within the studio system can make one self-conscious about throwing out ideas that might be considered off-the-wall. The experiences with Joe Papp were very special. I was new to theater and Joe had never done film, so he was the producer on **The Pirates of Penzance**, and I was the executive producer. It was really an honor to work with him. Credits, to me, have always been a means of barter to get films made.

Credits are very odd things in this business. The producer credit today has become so diffuse. Some films have a dozen or more producers on it. I think producers had a higher regard in the traditional studio system because the studios and the producers managed filmmaking. They hired the director and fired the director and it was managed in a whole different way. But I grew up during the period of the auteur theory, and the French New Wave, and the idea of the director and the producer being aligned was the way I've always looked at it. It was us against the world, not in opposition. There are producers, like Jerry Bruckheimer, Brian Grazer, and Joel Silver who still work in similar ways with the studios. I've always taken a different course from studio producers. Most the films I've done have been with writer-directors—that same relationship that I had going back to Paul Williams. That was a magic period, and I still try to emulate that. Working today with directors like Mary Harron is very satisfying. We had a great experience once [on **American Psycho**, 2000], and we try to work together and do it again. We just finished a film that was at the Venice Film Festival called **The Moth Diaries** (2011).

With each film I try to stretch the medium a little bit, not just do something because it's the fad of the moment. When you do a horror film with Brian De Palma, it can be pushing the genre in new ways. Right now, there's a tendency for the studios to do what they call branding. It's a mixed blessing. Psychologically, you try not to keep redoing things, but there's a practical attraction to it, whether you're doing a **Wall Street: Money** →

03 Pressman with Joseph Papp and Gail Merrifield Papp at Shepperton Studios in 1982 on the set of **The Pirates of Penzance**

04 Pressman with director Mary Harron on the set of **The Moth Diaries**, Montreal, Canada, 2010

05 Pressman and Harron also collaborated on **American Psycho** (2000) starring Christian Bale in a landmark performance

Edward R. Pressman | Interview 147

> "Being involved in making films excited me, and it still does. It's still fulfilling. Each film we make is a bit of a miracle."

Never Sleeps (2010) or a new **Crow** or **Bad Lieutenant**. To me, Werner Herzog's sequel of **Bad Lieutenant** stands on its own because he wasn't trying to do the same thing—Werner never saw Abel Ferrara's original (1992). A film like that is easier to get made, because it had a predecessor, versus doing something new like **The Moth Diaries**. In this age of branding—remakes, sequels, and tentpole properties—there are still ways of being inventive.

What's happening now more than ever is a renaissance in the world of television and, therefore, a gravitation of major actors and filmmakers to television. We've been approached to do series. Fox would like to do a **Wall Street** TV series, we're developing a series based on the **Mutant Chronicles** (2008) property, another company approached us about doing a **Bad Lieutenant** TV series. Up until now, we've only done one TV series with **The Crow**, when PolyGram was in business, but now we're looking at it more seriously.

There are all kinds of new trends happening, such as the enormous growth of film in the Asian market. That's the most dynamic place in the world right now. So some of the things we're doing involve filmmakers who have an interest in subjects that might appeal to that part of the

01 Bad Lieutenant (1992), directed by Abel Ferrara

02 Bad Lieutenant: Port of Call—New Orleans (2009), directed by Werner Herzog

> "There are all kinds of new trends happening, such as the enormous growth of film in the Asian market. That's the most dynamic place in the world right now."

world. We have a buddy-action-comedy set in Hong Kong and India called **Bangalore Bullet**. In a similar way, the Latin market is very dynamic. We just optioned a comic book called *Feeding Ground*. It's printed in Spanish on one side and on the other in English. It's a comic book with political undercurrents, which I think will have appeal because it's like **Jaws** on the desert. Illegal immigrants who cross Devil's Highway from Mexico into the USA must contend with werewolves. The companies that are very interested in it are companies we've never dealt with before, but they're either aligned with the studios or Latin broadcasters that are very substantial. They're looking to do projects with international appeal; it could be in English as well as Spanish. As an independent company, we're always looking for new ways of finding financing that works within the same creative parameters. That's always part of the game, to try to find new ways to get films made.

LEGACY

Erich Pommer

Born in 1889, Erich Pommer was Berlin's very own "boy wonder," a producer whose impact at UFA Studios in the early 1920s matched that of Irving Thalberg at MGM a few years later. From **The Cabinet Of Dr. Caligari** (1920) to **Dr. Mabuse: The Gambler** (1922), from **The Last Laugh** (1924) to **Metropolis** (1927), he oversaw the films that won German cinema an international reputation for the first time.

The young Alfred Hitchcock, who worked at UFA in the early 1920s and whose 1939 film **Jamaica Inn** was produced by Pommer, recalled being astounded by the sheer scale of the studio operation put in place by the German producer. "The studio where I worked was tremendous, bigger than Universal is today. They had a complete railroad station built on the back-lot. For a version of **Siegfried**, they built the whole forest of the Nibelungenlied," Hitchcock stated.

Pommer wasn't scared of spending vast amounts on prestige films. There are many stories about his working relationship with Fritz Lang, whose career he kickstarted. Lang would always ask for extra resources. Pommer would always resist before eventually deciding that, yes, the investment was worthwhile. This wasn't weakness, but more an acknowledgement that giving the best directors their creative freedom was the best way to build the UFA brand.

"The young, fanatically striving UFA chief," as director Ludwig Berger called him, was equally interested in the technical, business, and artistic side of filmmaking. At the same time he was encouraging Lang, F.W. Murnau, and E.A. Dupont to make ambitious movies aimed at the international market, he was also producing populist fare for German audiences.

Directors had complete confidence in him and did their best work under him. He challenged them—"please invent something new, even if it's crazy," he told Murnau and his team as they began work on **The Last Laugh**—but gave them the resources they needed to excel. As Patrick McGilligan notes in his biography of Lang, the notoriously combustible German director fell out with almost every producer that he ever worked with. Pommer was the one boss Lang always accepted. "In fact, Pommer's sterling

01 Erich Pommer (1930)

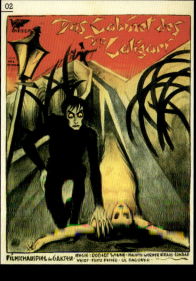

example ultimately became a chink in Lang's psychology, an obstacle to his acceptance of any other, lesser figure in that position." Pommer was prepared to back the most oblique projects. Few other producers of his status would have supported a film as odd as **The Cabinet of Dr. Caligari** or agreed to it being shot in such a wildly expressionistic style.

"If by interesting lighting or focusing on the stairs or populating the scene with the right faces one can lend a touch of high style to a crummy bar patronized by thieves and whores, as, for instance, the old Dutch paintings do, then the crummy bar can emanate as much art as a Gothic cathedral can," the producer of **Dr. Mabuse: The Gambler**—the perfect example of an art-house gangster film—wrote in the trade press in 1922 (quoted in Klaus Kreimeier's *The UFA Story*.) "It is immaterial what subject one chooses for making an artistic film. The only essential condition is that it be made by artists who know what the public wants, but also know what they themselves want."

In the 1920s, when Pommer was in his heyday, he was as celebrated as any of his directors. Almost a century later, his name doesn't have the currency that it once did. There are historical and critical reasons why he has been consigned to the margins of film history. Later writers, extolling the genius of Lang and Murnau, don't always acknowledge his contribution to their work. He left UFA for the first time in 1926, when there was huge alarm at the studios about the soaring cost of **Metropolis**. Amid the mounting financial problems, Pommer resigned and migrated briefly to Hollywood. Although he returned in 1927, and then played a pivotal role as German movies adjusted to sound as well as producing several more classic films—among them **Asphalt** and **The Blue Angel**—he never regained the power he had once held.

A German-Jew, Pommer was wise enough to head into exile with his family when the Nazis came to power in 1933. The following 30 years were hardly uneventful. He worked in Britain, in Hollywood again, took American citizenship, went back to Germany after World War II to reorganize the film industry and then spent his retirement in California. Nonetheless, nothing in his subsequent career matched the glory days at UFA. In his prime, Pommer revolutionized German cinema. As UFA historian Kreimeier wrote, he "kept in touch with every aspect of the industry—business policy and artistic ideas, technical challenges and organizational duties, the tastes of both the masses and the avant-garde. In the context of Germany, he was the first modern film producer. Like no one else of his time, he understood the new medium's special qualities and knew how to coordinate its commercial and artistic aspects...he was the great pioneer." Pommer died in 1966.

02 The Cabinet of Dr. Caligari (1920)

03 Metropolis (1927)

04 The Last Laugh (192

Lauren Shuler Donner

"When it comes to material it's about good story and good characters, but as a producer you also have to look ahead. You have to feel the temperature of the country and understand where the next trend will be. It can lead you to clues about what kind of movie to develop. I'm a news junkie. I read a lot of magazines and a lot of newspapers. You can get so secluded in Hollywood."

X-Men Origins: Wolverine (2009)

Versatile and enduring, Lauren Shuler Donner stands among the leading producers working in Hollywood today. Her movies have resonated critically and commercially—raking in billions at the box office worldwide—while several also have become defining films of their particular decade.

Shuler Donner's first feature film, comedy **Mr. Mom** (1983), developed from an original idea by writer John Hughes, was a break-out success and helped launch both Hughes' and actor Michael Keaton's movie careers. She went on to produce 1980s favorites such as Joel Schumacher's **St. Elmo's Fire** (1985), Hughes' **Pretty in Pink** (1986), and **Ladyhawke** (1985). The latter, starring Michelle Pfeiffer, was directed by her then husband-to-be, Richard Donner, with whom she now runs production shop The Donners' Company.

In the 1990s, with a producer deal at Warner Bros., Shuler Donner made political comedy **Dave** with director Ivan Reitman, and also produced whale adventure movie **Free Willy** (which spawned sequels and a TV series). Both films were box-office highlights of 1993. They were followed by more standouts, including Nora Ephron's romantic comedy **You've Got Mail** (1998), starring Meg Ryan and Tom Hanks, and Oliver Stone's football drama **Any Given Sunday** (1999). Among Shuler Donner's executive producer credits is Warren Beatty's hip-hop political satire **Bulworth** (1998).

In the next decade, Shuler Donner ramped up the comic book-based **X-Men** franchise, which has yielded multiple sequels and spin-offs for Twentieth Century Fox. The producer also managed to work on movies such as Southern period drama **The Secret Life of Bees** (2008) and family comedy **Hotel for Dogs** (2009).

Entering her fourth decade as a film producer, Shuler Donner has various projects percolating. Among them, an **X-Men: First Class** sequel, as well as **The Wolverine** (2013), starring Hugh Jackman.

INTERVIEW

Lauren Shuler Donner

"My strength is understanding the story and getting that story to the screen, and everything that is involved with that. Understanding that you need original characters that are complicated, that come to life, that are unique unto themselves; and a story that is not predictable, that has twists and turns, and complexities. The real sign of a good producer is when you have an idea and you hire a writer, and they turn in that first draft and it stinks—if you can fix it, you're a good producer. Same thing applies in the editing room. It's just not that easy.

The other thing you need as a producer is people skills. Basically, what you're doing as a producer is convincing other people to do what you think is right for the movie. Convincing the director to try another take, maybe with humor this time. And saying to the studio, "This scene is so crucial to the story, we need more money." You're convincing everybody to do what you believe is best for the movie, and guiding that ship to the screen. It's also about learning how to get people to do what's best for the movie. Is it by making them laugh or yelling at them? You have to be a little bit fearless, but also aware of what's going on politically. It's such a big machine; there are so many people involved. It's such a collaborative effort.

You also have to be the peacemaker. The cinematographer cares about their lights, and the production designer cares about their set. It's about getting them to work together in harmony so that they're not fighting each other. Getting the cinematographer not to dominate the young new director or firing the composer because it's just not working, or whatever the movie needs.

When it comes to material it's about good story and good characters, but as a producer you also have to look ahead. You have to feel the temperature of the country and understand where the next trend will be. It can lead you to clues about what kind of movie to develop. I'm a news junkie. I read a lot of magazines and a lot of newspapers. You can get so secluded in Hollywood. I think one of the reasons I am successful is that I am from Cleveland, Ohio. When someone pitches me something, I often say, "In Cleveland, Ohio, they don't care about that." A lot of people come from New York and Los Angeles and their ideas are so sophisticated they don't reach the heart of the country.

I majored in film at Boston University, and then came out to Los Angeles. I didn't know anybody and just knocked on doors. I actually started working in medical and educational films at a company called Wexler Films, run by Sy Wexler. I talked my way into a job there doing A/B rolling, where you take the original negative and marry it to the work print. It's unbelievable that they'd let a kid come in and touch the original film, but there was a terrific woman there who worked with me. Three months into my job as an editor, a woman I'd spoken with at NBC called me and asked if I wanted to come in and work in their vacation relief program. I was one of the token women: it was three women and 300 men—this is in the 1970s. It was all technical jobs: I pulled cable, I learned videotape editing. I figured out that camera [operating] would be the best thing I could do there, because that's what got me into film initially. In college, I was very into photography, as well as writing.

So I asked the guys who worked on **The Tonight Show** how to work the camera, and then asked to be moved to the local station, because I knew they'd never let me start on a national show. I shot the news and local shows, and I then started to freelance as a camera operator. I shot everything—sitcoms, game shows, commercials, movies on tape. After three years, I became an associate producer in television. I knew everybody from freelancing, so I could basically crew the shows and help write them.

Then an interesting twist of fate happened: I was in a major car accident. A woman ran a red light and I smashed into her. I had a concussion and shattered my kneecap. It laid me up for months and so I got let go. I started writing and found that I really liked writing and working with other writers. I was better as an editor and a collaborator than I was on my own. A friend told me about a job opening. Nancy Meyers was a

"Three months into my job as an editor, a woman I'd spoken with at NBC called me and asked if I wanted to come in and work in their vacation relief program. I was one of the token women: it was three women and 300 men—this is in the 1970s."

story editor at Motown Productions and was leaving to write. I came in and they were making **Thank God It's Friday** (1978)—they gave me the script and I gave them five pages of constructive criticism and they said, "Very good, you're hired." And that was that. I'd stay late and read Nancy's files, memorizing every agent and who they represented, because I had no clue. But I am very fast on my feet, so I learned it all very quickly. I won an associate producer on **Thank God It's Friday**. I then produced a movie for television that Joel Schumacher wrote and directed called **Amateur Night at the Dixie Bar and Grill** (1979). It was a very fun experience because we made it like a little feature, and it ended up being very well regarded.

By that point I was 28, and nervous to go out on my own and produce. So I joined another company with someone I ended up not respecting and I left. At that point, I realized I had really good relationships with writers and I had a decent story sense. I figured if I could set up five movies and I would get initial development money for those movies, I could live for a year. During that time, I read a very funny article in *National Lampoon* by John Hughes called *Kids*. He started off saying, "Lampoon wanted me to write about kids, so I knocked up my wife." I called him and we clicked. I think it was the Midwestern connection that sort of did it: John's from Chicago and I'm from Cleveland. At the time, he was working on a movie for ABC's feature division and he'd asked me to come onto that project. He was working from Chicago and would send me pages. One time, John called and told me that his wife Nancy had gone to Arizona and he had been left with his two boys. He was hopeless. He'd never been to a grocery store or operated a washing machine, because he and Nancy were together right out of college. He would tell me this stuff and I'd be on the floor laughing. He asked if I thought this could make a good movie. He said he had 80 pages in a drawer of a script called **Mr. Mom** (1983) and asked if I wanted to read it. I loved it and we finished the script. John was amazing. He would come to LA, I would give him notes, and he'd go outside my office to where my assistant Anne was. He'd say, "Anne, get up." And he'd sit down behind the typewriter and immediately write the pages. He wrote **Mr. Mom** in four weeks. We developed it on our own. I was brand new—this was my first feature. We were able to sell it to Paramount, found director Ted Kotcheff, and got it to Michael Keaton. Everybody said that it wasn't a movie; we believed it was, but we were →

MR. MOM

(01) Shuler Donner's first feature film, **Mr. Mom** (1983), was an unexpected hit. "It was very funny," she says, "because nobody believed in it. Fox distributed it domestically and they had another movie called **The Star Chamber** (1983) with Michael Douglas. That was their big summer movie and they were going to roll us out regionally and then let us die. But what happened was **The Star Chamber** died and we exploded. In two weeks, **The Star Chamber** was pulled and we rolled out into their theaters. Later, they called that their '**Mr. Mom** pattern' of rollouts—start in the West and roll East. But that's the wonderful thing about our business, we reinvent ourselves all the time."

X-MEN

(01–06) When Shuler Donner had a producer deal at Warner Bros., her development executive Scott Nimerfro (now a TV writer/showrunner) introduced her to Marvel Comics' *X-Men* superheroes. "Scott brought in the *X-Men* comics. I knew of them, but hadn't grown up reading them. My husband Dick [director Richard Donner] and I were going to Seattle that weekend, and I brought the book of bios of the main characters: Wolverine, Jean Grey, Cyclops, Professor Xavier, and Storm. I sat down and read the first one, Wolverine/Logan—immediately I thought this was unbelievable. They're psychologically complex, well-drawn characters. Especially Logan is a real tragic character—he doesn't have a memory, he's dealing with unrequited love, he's got things implanted in his body, he's got a 'beserker rage' he can't control. I was hooked. I read all the bios and started reading all the comics from the first years and then watched the first couple of years of the cartoons, so I would have a solid basis. We pitched the idea to Warners, but I think they didn't want to do it because they had a deal with DC Comics. So Dick and I went to Bill Mechanic, who was running Fox. I knew Bill from Disney. And he was a major *X-Men* fan—he sold his *X-Men* collection to pay for college. We were preaching to the choir. We brought in a writer, and he did a fantastic first draft, but it was way too expensive to make, so we couldn't do it. After Dick decided not to direct the first **X-Men**, Peter Rice, our executive at Fox, said, 'How about this guy Bryan Singer?' I'd seen **The Usual Suspects** (1995). I thought it was a good idea. He can do action, he has a great visual style, he's good with performance, and he can handle multiple characters. So we went to Bryan and started developing. It took years. At one point, we were prepping and we didn't have the script done—we didn't have the third act resolved at all. So we shut down, got it right, and then booted up again. It was a very long journey, but a very great one." **(02)** Shuler Donner and Patrick Stewart on set during filming. **(04)** Shuler Donner and Hugh Jackman bond on the set of the third **X-Men** film, **X-Men: The Last Stand** (2006). In 2012 they shot **The Wolverine** together. **(05)** From left to right: Actors Patrick Stewart and Ian McKellen, Shuler Donner, and director Bryan Singer on the set of **X2** (2003). **(06)** Shuler Donner and Hugh Jackman conferring behind the scenes of **X2**.

"Films are such a big machine; there are so many people involved. It's such a collaborative effort. You also have to be the peacemaker. The cinematographer cares about their lights, and the production designer cares about their set. It's about getting them to work together in harmony so that they're not fighting each other."

> "The real sign of a good producer is when you have an idea and you hire a writer, and they turn in that first draft and it stinks—if you can fix it, you're a good producer."

nervous. John had a TV deal with producer Aaron Spelling, so he thought if we brought Aaron on board, and if it didn't go as a feature, it could go as a TV series. But neither of us understood that Aaron didn't do comedy, and he actually turned out to be our nemesis. Aaron decided he didn't like our director and, in turn, Michael Eisner, who ran Paramount at the time, went sour on the project. I went running to Universal and Aaron went running to MGM. Aaron beat me, so MGM set it up and then Aaron proceeded to take my points and eventually kick John off the movie. Everybody has those situations and we continue to have them. It was a good learning experience for me and, still, the essence of the movie is there.

Concurrently, Anthea Sylbert at Warner Bros. gave me the script **Ladyhawke**, by Ed Khmara, as a writing sample. I read it and wanted to do it, and it got set up at Warners, but it took years to get made. Eventually I gave the script to [producer] Alan Ladd Jr., who gave it to [director] Richard Donner. Dick ultimately wanted to do it, but it would have been at the Ladd Company. Warners then had a huge hit with **Private Benjamin** (1980). So I went in on that Monday when everyone was in a good mood and said, "Please can I have my script back. You have hundreds of movies in development and I have this one. It'll be at a sister company, the Ladd Company. You guys will distribute it." They were in such a good mood, they gave it back to me. So I set it up with Laddie, we got Dick, and then the Ladd Company closed. We ended up back at Warners, and Warners split it with Fox. It took years to get the script right, there was a writers strike, and Dick went off and did another movie. So, ultimately, we got it together three years later, as **Mr. Mom** was being released.

Then Joel Schumacher called me and said he had a script called **St. Elmo's Fire** and asked if I would produce it. We made it at Columbia Pictures, which was a great experience. Then John [Hughes] called and said he had a script he wrote called **Pretty in Pink** and a brand new director, Howard Deutch, and would I produce it, which I did. John and I remained close. He really pushed Joel and I to look at Ally Sheedy, Judd Nelson, and Emilio Estevez, because he was so enamored with them from **The Breakfast Club** (1985). We looked at them and put them in **St. Elmo's Fire** (1985). And John used my crew from **Pretty in Pink** (1986) and rolled them right into **Ferris Bueller's Day Off** (1986).

Jeffrey Katzenberg then brought me in under contract at Disney. He left Paramount and during his first few years at Disney, he had this wonderful idea to put writers and producers together on →

01 St. Elmo's Fire (1985), directed by Joel Schumacher and with an all-star cast

02 Pretty in Pink (1986), directed by Howard Deutch

Moviemaking marriage

(05) "The secret to our company is that we don't work together as producer and director," Shuler Donner says of her production company with her husband, director Richard Donner. The Donners prefer to give each other support and, if they work together, it's mainly as executive producers. "It's been wonderful. He has helped me enormously. I learned a tremendous amount just watching him direct his movies. And I have the extra bonus of living with him."

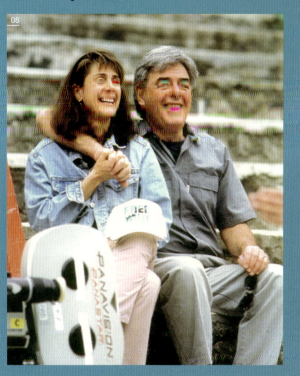

03 Dave (1993), director Ivan Reitman's political comedy starring Kevin Kline

04 Free Willy (1993), directed by Simon Wincer

YOU'VE GOT MAIL

(01–02) *You've Got Mail* (1998) was based on the novel (and 1940 film) *The Shop Around the Corner*. "Julie Durk, who worked for me, found it," remembers Shuler Donner. "She said, 'I found this good movie, but I don't know how to do it.' I looked at it and said I have an idea. I had just gotten online and was starting to figure out the internet. Amy Pascal [Production Executive], who was at Turner at the time, suggested [writer/director] Nora Ephron. We went to Nora and her sister Delia, and they wrote a great script. Then Warner Bros. bought Turner and the project moved to Warners." **(01)** Shuler Donner with Tom Hanks on set.

> "The film business is really different now. On a very personal and emotional level, it was more fun back then. Especially in the 1980s, there was more of a sense that you were making art, you were making film."

the first floor of the Animation Building at Disney. We would help each other and it was a really good relationship. I produced **Three Fugitives** (1989) there. I then left and went to Warners, and produced **Free Willy** and its sequel (1993, 1995), **Dave** (1993), **You've Got Mail** (1998), and **Any Given Sunday** (1999), among other films. The next decade I started with **X-Men** (2000), but balanced my life with children's movies **Hotel for Dogs** (2009), **She's the Man** (2006), and also **The Secret Life of Bees** (2008).

I don't have a deal at a particular studio now, but I have multiple movies set up, and that keeps me financed. Back in the 1980s and 1990s, studio producer deals were the thing. Everybody had deals, and you would bring material to your studio. Once I left Warners after ten years—because I was starting to make movies for Fox [**X-Men**] and other studios—I found that I was much more prolific. I would have multiple movies going at the same time. The film business is really different now. On a very personal and emotional level, it was more fun back then. Especially in the 1980s, there was more of a sense that you were making art, you were making film. We understood it was a business—and obviously I make commercial movies—but there was a camaraderie and an ethos of everybody, studios and filmmakers, in it together. My job was to partner with the director and the studio knew that, but I also knew where my bread was buttered. You'd basically do what was best for the movie. And as long as everything was going all right they left you alone. To the point where I remember saying to the studio: "Do you like our dailies?" "Yes." "Will you call our director and tell him?"

Now studios are owned by major corporations that they have to answer to. There is more of a culture of micro-managing, to the detriment of movies, because there are too many chefs and, inside of that, there is too much second-guessing. You have the presidents guessing what the chairman wants. Then you have what the producer and director want. It's not always a cohesive team and it should be. When it is, it's great. I love working for the studios as long as we're all making the same movie."

03 Shuler Donner and Gina Prince-Bythewood, the director of **The Secret Life of Bees**

04 The Secret Life of Bees (2008)

Lauren Shuler Donner | Interview

Jeremy Thomas

 "It's a strange calling, the movies, and not necessarily lucrative. It can be lucrative...but for very few. I know how fortunate I am. I want to continue making movies because I love it. And I feel I still have my hands enough in it so that I can continue forever. I don't think I'll have to give up."

Sexy Beast (2000)

Flash back to April 1988 at the 60th Academy Awards. British producer Jeremy Thomas, then in his late 30s, presides over an astonishing night for Bernardo Bertolucci's **The Last Emperor**. The film won nine Oscars including Best Picture, which Thomas himself received. A quarter of a century later, the London-based Thomas is as internationally minded as ever. One of the paradoxes about his career is that, as he has grown older, he has moved yet further away from the British filmmaking establishment rather than toward it. A compelling argument can be made that he is the most significant British producer since Michael Balcon—the former Ealing boss—but whereas Balcon famously made films "projecting Britain and the British character," Thomas is a born subversive. You'd never find him making **Passport to Pimlico** (1949) or one of the Doctor films that his father Ralph Thomas directed with such success in the 1950s. His territory is more J.G. Ballard and William Burroughs. He is drawn to working with the most visionary and perverse auteurs, such as Nicolas Roeg, David Cronenberg, Takashi Miike, Julien Temple, and of course, Bertolucci.

Born in 1949, Thomas is, by his own admission, a product of the 1960s. His personality and *modus operandi* are very different from those of younger British producers who emerged in the Thatcher era. He grew up around movies and has a reverence for film as an art that these successors, busy churning out rom-coms, conspicuously lack. When the Rank Organisation described Roeg's movie **Bad Timing** (1980) as "a sick film made by sick people for sick people," he saw it as a badge of honor. Thomas is a formidable businessman and has an intimate understanding of international sales. His contacts in Europe and Asia are unrivalled. Hollywood gives him its grudging respect, not just because of the Oscars, but because he is one of the few producers today whose credit, "Jeremy Thomas presents" regularly appears at the front of his films. Thomas has now been active as a producer for 40 years and remains as prolific as ever. His numerous credits include **The Shout** (1978), **Merry Christmas Mr. Lawrence** (1983), **The Hit** (1984), **Naked Lunch** (1991), and **Sexy Beast** (2000).

INTERVIEW

Jeremy Thomas

"What is a producer? An enabler...no films are made without a producer of sorts. In America, the producer is the studio. They [the studios] get people to produce the film as running interference with the talent. Then, in the studio are all the people who produce the film—the line producers, the production managers, the costume departments, all the departments are basically run by the studio and the studio does the production of the film. The producer is involved in another way. Then you have a group of super indies who have the knack for making big hits. With an entrepreneurial producer like me, I am trying to put many, many people together, and to control the whole idea. I am trying to share with many and have some imprimatur on the film, to keep some element of the film for myself. When I have "Jeremy Thomas Presents" on the credits, I do that because I want my colleagues to know that I've managed to finance my films and am proud of them.

When I was a child, a producer was an elegant woman in a mink coat, driving a convertible Aston Martin. That was Betty Box. I couldn't really understand what a director or a producer did. I think even today, many people don't understand what the producer does, although they understand what the director does. But I had these wonderful teachers. First of all, there was my dad [director Ralph Thomas]. I was exposed from the age of my first memories to the movies in the manufacturing sense, in the film sense. I'd see the passion and the downside.

I had some big mentors—obviously my father, my uncle Gerald [Thomas] and Betty Box [the producer partner of Ralph Thomas]. I saw them working. Betty was an extraordinary woman and the more I found out about her, the more extraordinary she became. I read her book, *Lifting the Lid: The Autobiography of Film Producer Betty Box*. During the war, she was writing, producing, and directing. All the men were on the Front. She was doing everything herself. This was a woman producer who produced 60 films. Few know her significance in British cinema today.

She [Box] and Ralph Thomas were a contract producer director team for Rank in their heyday. After that system finished, a lot of people weren't very good at transferring into the indie world. It was all more gentlemanly then, a different world, and a different time. Today's world is much more cut-throat and difficult in terms of funding films. When I started producing films, I would produce my films with two funders. It was much easier. Things started to get difficult in the mid-1990s. I had a certain pattern—pre-sell the film for more than it cost and then go into a movie broken even. That was the business plan. It was ideal. It was incredible luck because we had got hold of product that people wanted. I had more buyers than I needed. I had regular companies in Europe who wanted my movies. I had different distribution companies who were in business with me. There were more cinemas, more earning power. There was TV protection. When you'd done the film, you'd sell to TV. Then, VHS became a proper market and DVD became a proper market.

I became a producer by chance. Most of my life has been unplanned. I left school when I was 17. I got five O' levels. I wanted to go to work. I started in the laboratories and ended up at

01 Thomas with his director uncle Gerald Thomas in 1984

> "I don't like brutality in relationships. I must say I was a fairly soft mogul, a soft entrepreneur. I've been luckily successful, but I've been choosing films that are individual."

[production company] Good Times with Sandy Lieberson and David Puttnam via many jobs in the movie business on the way.

I'd been going in a direction to make movies, but it wasn't really clear to me until a certain point what I was doing. I was working in the cutting rooms, working as an assistant in different areas of the movie business. I got some breaks. I worked on fantastic films—**The Harder They Come** (1972), Ken Loach films, and with Ray Harryhausen. I got a break from Ken, editing a TV film for him. Then, **Brother, Can You Spare A Dime** (1975), which I edited, went to Cannes. Lieberson, who is a fantastic man, took me under his wing and exposed me to Hollywood and New York as an adult. He had been an important agent in LA and had many friends in New York. I went to New York to edit **Brother Can You Spare A Dime**. Many of my good friends today are from Sandy. I suddenly understood Hollywood. I was editing and intending to be a director. The director Philippe Mora said to me, why don't you come to Australia and edit and produce this film [**Mad Dog Morgan**, 1976]. He said he could get financing from the Australian Film Commission. I went to Australia with a handwritten letter from my father in a sealed envelope addressed to Sir Norman Rydge, who was head of Greater Union Films. He had distributed 30 or so of my father's films, although my father had never been to Australia to promote them. I got a letter back to meet Sir Norman at his club in Hyde Park, Sydney. He said, "Well, your father sent me a message that you want to make a film. We don't really invest in film, but you've no idea how much money your father has made for me. I've had so much money from the Doctor films and I've also made a lot of money from the Carry On films. I →

BAD TIMING

(02–03) "A sick film made by sick people for sick people," a Rank executive famously sneered at Nicolas Roeg's **Bad Timing** (1980). For Thomas, though, Roeg was one of the true masters—a filmmaker always probing away at "the strangeness of life and the strangeness of human relations." In the film, shot in Vienna, Art Garfunkel played Alex Lindon, a Freudian analyst who has an intense and destructive affair with a young American woman—Theresa Russell **(03)**. **(02)** From left to right: Thomas, Roeg, and cinematographer Anthony Richmond.

"At the beginning, I didn't know what the hell I was doing, but after a few movies, the clouds thinned out and it became clear. I understood what I was doing."

want you to go to see John Fraser tomorrow at British Empire Films."

The next day, I went to see John Fraser, who was a lovely guy. He said: "I've no idea why Sir Norman has done this, but I've been told to give you a third of the budget for your movie."

I didn't get to edit the film—it was such a nightmare to produce. Having Dennis Hopper, David Gulpilil, and Jack Thompson, and all those actors there—it was full-time work, with 120 speaking parts and six weeks (to make it). I realized what producing was! When I got the budget for shooting in Australia, a handwritten budget, my pencil went onto the budget form. How much should I put here? How much will the horses cost? That's how we did it. I was completely green. Then I was a producer. The film turned out pretty well, **Mad Dog Morgan**. It has become a celebrated piece of Australian film history. We took it to Cannes with the help of the AFDC [the Australian Film Development Corporation].

I went back to London having had a sniff of Cannes. We sold the film to an American distributor and got completely shafted! We didn't get any money. There were lawsuits and all that for years. I started learning—it was like learning by falling off the horse. When I went to London, I had a friend, Michael Austin, who had written a script. I persuaded him to let me produce it. This was **The Shout** (1978), adapted from a Robert Graves story. I took it to Jerzy Skolimowski. Another key figure in my career was Sir John Terry. He was a magnificent man. He ran the NFCC [National Film Finance Corporation]. He was a really amusing character with a bow tie. He liked me and he came into **The Shout**. There was a lot of controversy from my colleagues about a Polish director. Somehow, I managed to get it through.

The Recorded Picture Company—my company—was started in 1972. I wouldn't say I wanted to create a media empire. I was much more idealistic. I was influenced by the 1960s. I came of age between 1965 and 1970. There was a different ideology at the time than for the Thatcher children. You had a different feeling from what was instilled in you in later decades. That is still in my life today. I'd seen Sandy Lieberson and David Puttnam's company Good Times, where I had worked. I thought, I want to be like that. They all had a fantastic time, creating together, and working together. Other people have looked at my model and are doing the same. My advantage—and disadvantage—is that I am probably a decade older than anybody else [other British producers]. If you look at the ages, there is nobody between me at 62 and Tim [Bevan] and Eric [Fellner] at 52, and [Stephen] Woolley. There is a lost decade [between]. They've all crashed and burned, the colleagues from the beginning of my career.

I had a wonderful partner called Terry Glinwood who showed me the way. I was introduced to him by Sir John Terry. He had just finished working with Robert Stigwood. He knew everything about that beginning world of international film sales. He did some pre-sales →

01 The Shout (1978), directed by Jerzy Skolimowski and starring Alan Bates

Cronenberg connection

(02–03) Thomas met David Cronenberg in 1990, when **Bad Timing** was at the Toronto Film Festival and won a People's Choice award. The British producer was celebrating that award next to Cronenberg in the bar. Cronenberg mentioned that he wanted to make a film of *Naked Lunch* **(02)**. Thomas immediately decided he was the man to produce the movie. He knew Burroughs and his work, and very quickly set off to Lawrence, Kansas, to secure the film rights from the author. Thus began a creative relationship between Thomas and Cronenberg which has now lasted for more than 30 years. "When people hear Cronenberg's name, it's like a trademark for a super genre film—an attitude toward the body and going places where other people wouldn't take the camera. He's a beautiful filmmaker technically and a highly intelligent person," Thomas says of the Canadian director. **(03)** Kiera Knightley in **A Dangerous Method** (2011), also directed by Cronenberg and produced by Thomas.

THE LAST EMPEROR

(01–05) Thomas was only 38 years old when he won a Best Picture Oscar for **The Last Emperor**. The story of Puyi, the 12th Qing Emperor of China, who once ruled large swathes of the world, but ended his life as a humble gardener, was a daunting film to make. It required very delicate negotiations with the Chinese authorities as well as supreme organizational skills. This was storytelling on a truly epic scale. There was no CGI available, so the filmmakers could not take shortcuts with the set-pieces. They needed thousands of extras. What is even more astonishing is that the film was made without any US studio involvement.

"In China, making **The Last Emperor** was an enormous experience. It was ten percent of my life—four years, the whole thing, I was 38 years old. We found the money, made the movie. I had never been in China before."

MERRY CHRISTMAS MR. LAWRENCE

(01–04) Despite his very British background, Thomas is the most internationally-minded UK producer of his generation. He may not have spoken Japanese, but that didn't stop him from striking up an immediate rapport with Japanese auteur Nagisa Oshima when the two men first met at an event in Cannes. When Oshima later came to him and said he wanted to make a movie based on Laurens van der Post's experiences as a Japanese POW during World War II, Thomas leapt at the opportunity. **(03)** Thomas (left) with director Oshima (center) on location.

on **The Shout**. Then, Rank came in probably because of my family. The film was made and it was baffling to everybody, but it won the Grand Prix in Cannes.

Every single thing that happened on that film I was involved in. We had Robert Shaw and then two weeks before shooting, he came out of the film. One of the only actors approved was Alan Bates. He was in New York and about to go on the QE2 the next day. He had a ten-day journey back here, but we persuaded him on ship-to-shore radio to be in the film. He committed two days out of New York. It was my first experience of making films with the quality of English production. I had a great line producer, Joyce Herlihy. She was older than me and a very experienced person. She worked with me on many films after that. We had a very good crew, a fabulous crew. No man is an island. I had a wonderful group who looked after me— wonderful technicians who gravitated to me. I had a group with me for a decade or 20 years.

"I became a producer by chance. Most of my life has been unplanned. I left school when I was 17. I got five O' levels."

I had a very good run. I had **The Shout**, **Eureka** (1983), **Bad Timing**, **The Great Rock 'n' Roll Swindle** (1980), **Merry Christmas Mr. Lawrence** (1983). I also had a wonderful lawyer, Simon Olswang. I had a great sales agent, Terry Glinwood, helping me with his smarts in setting up films.

After **The Shout**, I was approached by Sandy [Lieberson] at Fox who asked, "do you want to produce Russ Meyer, Malcolm McLaren, and The Sex Pistols in this film written by Johnny Speight?" Did I ever! Other colleagues in the film business told me, "you'll never work again." I was told you can't do that, The Sex Pistols were really hot potatoes at that time. I engaged in that, which lasted three years after Russ Meyer was fired. Princess Grace [who was a board member at Fox] heard there was a film about The Sex Pistols. They had a board meeting. I heard [it may be apocryphal] that she was absolutely incensed that the management were making a film with Russ Meyer about The Sex Pistols.

With Nagisa Oshima, he came to me. I sat next to him at the award ceremony at Cannes when he won Best Director for **Empire of Passion** (1978). That was the year of **The Shout** [in Cannes]. We exchanged business cards. I spoke no Japanese. We had a lot of wine and were happy. Some years later, I got this script from him, a long script. He said he wanted to make this prisoner-of-war film written by Laurens van der Post, can you help me make it? By that time, I was fully aware of the extraordinary nature of Oshima's art and what a major, mind-blowing filmmaker he was. Again, with Terry Glinwood, we worked out a plan of how we were going to make the film—**Merry Christmas Mr. Lawrence**.

After **Merry Christmas Mr. Lawrence**, I knew the Peploes [Mark and Clare Peploe] in London from my social group. I'd met Bernardo [Bertolucci] maybe a couple of times at parties. I'd never thought that I was going to work with him. This was Bernardo Bertolucci of **Last Tango in Paris** (1972), **1900** (1976), and **The Conformist** (1970). I felt how would I work with somebody like that? In England, we don't really feel about our directors like that, but I felt people like Bertolucci were masters. Bertolucci rang me and said he wanted to meet. He was making a film. I met him in a Chinese restaurant and that was how it started. We liked each other very much. You can't find a better collaborator.

I was much younger when I was making films like **The Last Emperor** and **The Sheltering Sky** (1990). Of course, I could make those films today with a budget, but making these films was like trying to make a silk purse out of a sow's ear—they were a challenge. Those were really challenging movies, made in challenging physical situations with lots of different nationalities. In China, making **The Last Emperor** was an enormous experience. It was ten percent of my life—four years, the whole thing, I was 38 →

05 **Eureka** (1983), directed by Nicolas Roeg, and starring Gene Hackman

"I think even today, many people don't understand what the producer does, although they understand what the director does. But I had these wonderful teachers."

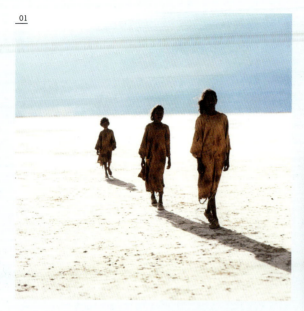

years old. We found the money, made the movie. I had never been in China before. It was the same with the Sahara [on **The Sheltering Sky**] and Bhutan [with **Little Buddha**, 1993]. You're going with 200 or 300 people under your control, your responsibility. You have to feed them, clothe them, and they were difficult places.

Most of the people in my career I've stayed close to. People are very difficult in films…always! That goes with the territory. If you're going to take umbrage with everybody who is difficult in the movies, you are going to have no friends left in the world. Everybody behaves badly—or most people behave badly. You make allowances for that. Obviously, I've behaved with some sort of decisiveness, but I try to behave in a fair and kind way because I want repeat business from everybody! I don't like brutality in relationships. I must say I was a fairly soft mogul, a soft entrepreneur. I've been luckily successful, but I've been choosing films that are individual. I am not choosing genre films. I'm not saying let's make a rom-com. At the beginning, I didn't know what the hell I was doing, but after a few movies, the clouds thinned out and it became clear. I understood what I was doing. I had luckily chosen good people to work with, people with more knowledge than me in areas that I didn't know about, and I learned from them. I am still in the learning game. How long can someone remain on the top of the pile and be prolific and in the zeitgeist? I've remained there for nearly 40 years.

A lot of producers in England are looking to produce films in England. I am looking to produce a movie and then, if it's in England, that's

01 Rabbit-Proof Fence (2002), directed by Phillip Noyce

02 Tideland (2005), directed by Terry Gilliam

03 13 Assassins (2010), directed by Takashi Miike

Working with Bertolucci

(01–06) Bertolucci famously called Thomas a hustler in the fur of a teddy bear. "That's because I used to have a coat made of fake furry material. It was made of furry material. It was beautiful, long, and double-breasted. That's why he thought it was a teddy bear coat. Bernardo always speaks in a very poetic way," Thomas later clarified the remark. The two first met in a Chinese restaurant in London. Thomas was in awe of Bertolucci's earlier movies like **The Conformist**, **Last Tango in Paris**, and **1900**, and relished the opportunity to work with the Italian on such grandiose projects as **The Last Emperor**, (04) **The Sheltering Sky**, and **Little Buddha**. The work wasn't easy. These were "challenging films made in challenging physical situations and with lots of different nationalities." Nonetheless, Thomas still describes Bertolucci as the ideal collaborator. (05) Thomas (left) with Keanu Reeves (center) and Bertolucci (right) during the filming of **Little Buddha**. (06) **The Dreamers** (2003) also directed by Bertolucci.

cool. I haven't done that many films in England.

I'd worked with Ken [Loach], Tony [Garnett], and those guys from Kestrel Films. They had the support to make these very radical films at the time. They had an office building, a great vibe, and we had a good time making movies. It's important that everybody engages and enjoys the magic of this exclusive and rarefied world that we live in. It's a strange calling, the movies, and not necessarily lucrative. It can be lucrative… But for very few. I know how fortunate I am. I want to continue making movies because I love it. And I feel I still have my hands enough in it so that I can continue forever. I don't think I'll have to give up. "

Ron Yerxa & Albert Berger

"Producing is easy to mystify. Different producers do different things, and different skills or abilities are appropriate at different times. There's no one approach. What's important is that a producer remains very flexible and mindful of what a specific situation requires."

Little Miss Sunshine (2006)

Producers Ron Yerxa and Albert Berger have a knack for making hybrid films—independently-minded projects that find their way into the studio system. They're drawn to unique, personal points of view that provoke, but also speak to wider audiences. They've made the first studio films of indie auteurs Steven Soderbergh (**King of the Hill**, 1993) and Alexander Payne (**Election**, 1999); adaptations such as Anthony Minghella's **Cold Mountain** (2003); and festival darlings-cum-Oscar-nominees, such as **Little Miss Sunshine** (2006).

Berger, a Columbia University film-school graduate who spent a decade working as a screenwriter in LA, says he became a producer out of frustration. "As a screenwriter you could get hired to write things, but they weren't necessarily movies that you want to go and see, let alone make," he says. "Then you were kept outside of the process once it did get made. It seemed very divorced from filmmaking. Producing was never something I thought about until that point."

Yerxa says he never had any ambition to work in the film business, but a willy-nilly path eventually led him to producing. After graduating from Stanford, he did a wide variety of things before becoming a film executive at CBS and Sovereign Pictures. Berger and Yerxa met in 1982 in Chicago through a mutual friend and banded together roughly ten years later to make their first feature with Soderbergh and form their company Bona Fide Productions. Yerxa describes the way he and Berger work together as "benign anarchy," because they don't have set roles or divisions of labor.

In 2012, the producers wrapped **The Necessary Death of Charlie Countryman**, starring Shia LaBeouf, and saw the release of **Ruby Sparks**, from **Little Miss Sunshine** directors Jonathan Dayton and Valerie Faris. They're preparing Alexander Payne's next film, **Nebraska** (2013), as well as Norwegian director Joachim Trier's **Louder Than Bombs**.

INTERVIEW

Ron Yerxa & Albert Berger

"We officially joined forces and started our company when we made Steven Soderbergh's **King of the Hill** (1993). We'd been friends for many years and recognized that the kinds of movies we responded to were very similar. So we decided to throw our lot in with each other just before the Sundance Film Festival in 1989. We stumbled into the first screening of Soderbergh's **Sex, Lies, and Videotape**, and approached Soderbergh afterward. That conversation turned into our first film **King of the Hill**. Steven still had to make **Kafka** (1991), so we took jobs at other film companies and waited for him to be ready. We shot **King of the Hill** in St. Louis, where we dressed two city blocks to look like the Depression era. Soderbergh has a unique style. He wanted austere conditions—windowless offices with simple tables, and electric wires all around. The funkier the better. We all stayed downtown in a converted railroad station that became a hotel. We would walk two blocks to an abandoned opera house/hockey stadium that we had taken over as the production offices and sound stage. It was a fun way to make a film. Universal bought the film as a negative pick-up, and as a result there wasn't any studio oversight. On that particular project, a theme emerged for us: We wanted to make idiosyncratic studio movies. That's rare, because normally you're making an independent film or you're making a studio film. **King of the Hill** was an exception to what Universal usually did and it was really because of Soderbergh. They completely believed in him based on **Sex, Lies, and Videotape** and were willing to take a chance on this film.

At the same time, another approach emerged for us: Producing the first studio film of a director who had made a name for himself in the independent world. We always look toward the independents for emerging filmmakers, trying to find people with a real voice, and then we look for the right way to team up with a studio. With Soderbergh, that's just the way it happened and we were the beneficiaries of that circumstance. Later on, it became a strategy that we kept going back to: Alexander Payne's **Election** (1999), Todd Field's **Little Children** (2006), David Siegel and Scott McGehee's **Bee Season** (2005), and Jonathan Dayton and Valerie Faris' **Ruby Sparks** (2012). We've been really fortunate that the directors we've worked with and the types of movies we've made are often the lucky few that studios are willing to take a chance on. And they've allowed us to make these movies in the way we intended. So we haven't really had that experience of people taking over the movie, or people behaving badly, or not being there for the right reasons. The kinds of movies we are interested in producing are often the same films that also speak personally to actors and filmmakers. These are small, personal movies that everybody appreciates making. Of course, some films have been difficult to get made, but most of them, regardless of the commercial outcome of the film, seem to get made without a lot of trauma and nightmares.

You have to look at each project and figure out how best to support the film. It's all about the movie, so that dictates the approach, as well as which people to bring onto the project. The key relationships are with the director and the line

01 Ron Yerxa (left) and Albert Berger (right) in Venice, Italy, around 1987 as they were formulating plans for their future production company

02 King of the Hill (1993), directed by Soderbergh

producer. Both of those are very important early decisions that a producer has to make—the director first and foremost. A lot of the directors we've worked with—like Steven Soderbergh, Alexander Payne, Todd Field and Anthony Minghella—absolutely know what they're doing. They're producorial and the production becomes very much a collaboration. With a line producer, you want somebody who's going to set the right tone on the production side and not just protect the budget at all costs.

Producing is easy to mystify. Different producers do different things, and different skills or abilities are appropriate at different times. There's no one approach. What's important is that a producer remains very flexible and mindful of what a specific situation requires. You could lay

"There are ten or 20 movie stars that all studios want to work with and they're the secret weapon. If they want to do a film that isn't exactly the studio's idea of a commercial enterprise, it still gets done due to their box-office powers."

down a rule, for example, that the script must be locked before going into production. But sometimes there are occasions where that just doesn't happen, or can't happen, and you have to reformulate things. It's sort of like a GPS on a car trip. When you take the wrong turn, it's fun to see that there's a whole other route to get where you're going. That fluid flexibility is a great thing.

The Switch (2010) was a project on which →

ELECTION

(01–02) Berger and Yerxa call social comedy **Election** (1999) "the best example of what we like to do." The film—a battle of wills between a frustrated teacher (Matthew Broderick) and an ambitious high-school student running for class president (Reese Witherspoon)—was based on an unpublished novel by Tom Perrotta, whom the producers had met on the recommendation of a friend. "We really responded to the book," says Berger. "It was provocative and written in many different characters' voices. Tracy Flick was a character unlike any we'd seen." They brought the project to David Gale, who was running MTV Films at the time. Gale thought it was very much in line with what MTV Films wanted to do under their deal with Paramount, and agreed to option the book with Berger and Yerxa serving as producers. The producers had had their eye on director Alexander Payne, who had just finished **Citizen Ruth** (1996). "Ron and I became very enamoured with the idea of bringing him and his writing partner Jim Taylor onto this project," says Berger. But it took until the premiere of **Citizen Ruth** at the Sundance Film Festival for the studio to be sold on Payne and Taylor. "Alexander is the type of director who makes a particular type of movie," adds Berger. "On the other hand, Paramount had this agenda to service a specific demographic that was not necessarily of interest to Alexander."

The studio saw it as a raucous comedy about high school, while the filmmakers thought of it as a subversive film about the implied resentment and warfare between teachers and students, as well as husbands and wives. "The great thing was that at some point MTV recognized it wasn't going to be the movie they'd thought it would

be, but loved the project anyway and decided to support the filmmakers. Paramount had a strong point of view about casting. Names such as Tom Hanks or Tom Cruise were brought up," remembers Berger. "Eventually it got to Matthew Broderick, who we were all excited about, including Paramount. Then they left us alone to make the movie." But the hybrid indie-studio project became somewhat problematic when the time came to prepare the film for release. "Paramount started deliberating what kind of film it was and how they'd market and sell it," says Yerxa. "There was a year that the film remained in this nether-territory because there was a controversy over the way it ended. The studio was advocating for an upbeat ending where the two characters become content in their life and jobs, which really wasn't the point of the film. So eventually Alexander and Jim came up with a great idea that, on the surface, satisfied the studio agenda. Matthew Broderick's character ends up teaching in the Museum of Natural History, and Reese Witherspoon's character achieves success as a Senator's aid." In the end, the producers credit Paramount head Sherry Lansing for rescuing the film. "It was one of those happy stories where it got a good release and a lot of critical acclaim," says Yerxa.

01–02 *The Switch* (2010), starring Jennifer Aniston and Jason Bateman

we had to use everything we'd learned up to that point to try to wrestle it toward a good conclusion. There were many last-minute changes that forced us to improvise. It came to us at a time when the film industry was changing a lot, and the kinds of movies that we were making seemed impossible to make. This was much more of a studio film for us. It went into turn-around from Sony and ended up at a production company, Mandate Pictures. For a variety of reasons, Mandate had a desire to make the movie before all the pieces were in place. There was some rethinking on the casting front that →

Credit where credit is due

(03–04) Little Miss Sunshine was the breakout success story of the 2006 Sundance Film Festival. The independently made dark comedy sold to distributor Fox Searchlight for just over $10 million. The film's good fortune continued all the way to the Academy Awards the following year, where it received four nominations, including Best Picture. But due to the Academy's rules limiting the producer credit to three people, Berger and Yerxa missed out on receiving an official nomination, despite being the first producers involved in the project and seeing it all the way through.

Struggles over credit aren't unusual in the producing world. It takes a village to produce a film, often with creative as well as financial producers vying for the coveted "producer" label. Five producers made **Little Miss Sunshine** – Berger, David Friendly, Peter Saraf, Marc Turtletaub, and Yerxa – while just three could receive the Oscar nomination at the time. The Oscar-winning script by Michael Arndt had come to Berger and Yerxa, who brought it to Turtletaub and his then-production partner Friendly, to produce and finance. Berger and Yerxa brought in directors Jonathan Dayton and Valerie Faris, and the four producers set the film up at Focus Features. Focus ultimately didn't make the film, and Turtletaub had since started a new company with Saraf, taking the producer tally to five.

"Given that, once the movie was getting made, we all did everything that we could in our power to fit in well together and to contribute and to support the movie," says Berger. "And so it wasn't one of those situations where there were financiers or tag-along producers who weren't involved. Everyone was as engaged as they should have been. Sometimes there are a lot of you and most of you aren't doing anything, and once in a while there are a lot of you and everybody joins together to make it work, and this was one of those examples. It was just unfortunate that, at the time, the Academy rules were such that they had to make a decision, but there was no fair or thorough way to make that decision."

"Thankfully they've changed the rules since then," says Yerxa. All five producers were credited by the Producers Guild of America, which has taken an increasingly prominent role in arbitrating credit decisions.

"One of the great things about film is that you collaborate with many people with different ideas. As a producer, you're central to trying to blend all of that together. Given that we're often the first people involved in trying to take something that's written and turn it into a movie, we have a very strong point of view about what we want to do."

"The kinds of movies we are interested in producing are often the same films that also speak personally to actors and filmmakers. These are small, personal movies that everybody appreciates making."

threw the whole premise of the movie into question. So we really had to scramble. **The Switch** was originally about an odd-looking guy who is infatuated with his beautiful best friend. She decides to have a child and he very much wants to help her in that effort. But instead she enlists him to help find a sperm donor. For various reasons, Jason Bateman got cast as the best friend. But there's absolutely nothing odd-looking about Bateman and, in fact, a lot of women would love to be his partner. So that created a panic. Within eight weeks, we had to adjust the script to jive with the new casting. Everything on that movie became about the writer [Allan Loeb] trying to rewrite under the guidance of the directors [Josh Gordon and Will Speck]. Then a new studio came into play, when Mandate sold the distribution rights to Miramax a week before production started. Miramax had a whole set of notes that they wanted addressed, which didn't get to us until the film had already started shooting.

It was a think-on-your-feet experience—almost like making a John Cassavetes film, but in the guise of a studio movie. Ultimately, through a lot of improvisation and hard work on everyone's part, we were able to pull something together that we were really happy with. I wouldn't say that this is how we normally make a film, but we were certainly able to use our experience to help guide this movie. In most cases, we generate our own projects. Either we'll find a book, an article or a script that doesn't have a director attached. Our whole thing is to try to make the film and protect that film. The easiest times are when you bring in a director and you're just completely in sync and you just let them do their thing. It also can get much more complicated because, as these projects evolve, you're not necessarily there just to protect the director's vision. Sometimes the studio or the financier or the writer or an actor has a very valid point. One of the great things about film is that you collaborate with many people with different ideas. As a producer, you're central to trying to blend all of that together. Given that we're often the first

01 Nicole Kidman and Jude Law in Anthony Minghella's epic **Cold Mountain** (2003)

02 Yerxa (left) and Berger high above the town of Brasov, Romania, where most of **Cold Mountain** was filmed

people involved in trying to take something that's written and turn it into a movie, we have a very strong point of view about what we want to do.

Another great collaboration was **Cold Mountain** (2003), which was material we found after the book had been published. It had been rejected by the studios at the manuscript stage and we were fortunate enough to see it the first week it came out in bookstores. We both read it and were able to convince the agent, Lynn Pleshette, to allow us a brief window to try to set it up. We thought Sydney Pollack would be a good director for it. We brought it to his company Mirage. At the time, Pollack was involved with **Eyes Wide Shut** (1999) and couldn't read it right away. Anthony Minghella was working on a project at Mirage, and the company's production head, Bill Horberg, thought he'd be a good guy to direct the film. **Cold Mountain** was a remarkable experience for us because every single person involved—the DoP, the costume designer, the editor, the production designer—was at the top of their profession. Minghella had won an Academy Award for **The English Patient** (1996) and worked with absolutely the best crews in the world. He was a fantastic writer and director, and we had an amazing cast. He was the most democratic guy we've ever worked with—

03 Little Children (2006), directed by Todd Field and starring Kate Winslet and Patrick Wilson

> "**Cold Mountain** was a remarkable experience for us because every single person involved—the DoP, the costume designer, the editor, the production designer—was at the top of their profession."

generous, collaborative, and open to everybody. We have had production deals with studios particularly when they had independent arms, including at Paramount, Warner Independent, Focus Features, and New Line. We look back very fondly on those years. The one place we've never had a deal, ironically, is Fox Searchlight, although that's the place where our taste is the most compatible. The changes in the business have been tough and unfortunate. There are still places that are making the kinds of movies that we make, and our projects are spread among them. Some of our projects are clearly in the right places and some aren't. Part of the reason for that is the residual effect of the independent divisions of studios closing down. We had projects at Paramount Classics, which became Paramount Vantage, which now is big Paramount. We had projects with Warner Independent and now they're at Warner Brothers. So, in those situations we're trying to feel our way toward their new sweet spot. Studios all want to make some of these smaller, personal movies—but not very many. The question is how does your project become one of the three such films that they'll make. The odds are getting tougher. It used to be

01-02 Ruby Sparks (2012), starring Zoe Kazan, Paul Dano, Annette Bening, and Antonio Banderas

that you were vying to be one of eight when there were entire divisions dedicated to these types of movies.

Many contradictions in the studio-versus-indie-film space have become all the more intense. Obviously, studios still make films with movie stars, even if they're character-driven stories, but they also want to make a lot of tentpole movies for younger audiences. We're really in such a time of accelerated evolution where there are micro films and huge $200-million studio films, while the areas that seem to be dying out are the social comedies and dramas. On the other hand, there are ten or 20 movie stars that all studios want to work with and they're the secret weapon. If they want to do a film that isn't exactly the studio's idea of a commercial enterprise, it still gets done due to their box-office powers. There's a lot of dodging and weaving between and among all these changes where, in ten years, it's going to look radically different from now. We're trying to make some of these films while there's still a crack in the door."

03 Berger (left) and Yerxa (right) confer with writer-actress Zoe Kazan on the set of Fox Searchlight's **Ruby Sparks**. The film reteamed the producers with their **Little Miss Sunshine** directors Jonathan Dayton and Valerie Faris. The film, about a novelist who wills his dream girl into existence by writing about her, was shot in LA during the summer of 2011 and opened in US theaters in July 2012

LEGACY

Alexander Korda

In Jeffrey Dell's 1939 satirical novel *Nobody Ordered Wolves*, the great Hungarian-born film producer Alexander Korda (1893–1956) is caricatured as Napoleon Bott, head of Paradox Film Productions. Bott is a cigar-chomping magnate—"an arresting figure with an immense cigar…anything from forty to sixty" —who trails chaos in his wake. By the end of the book, wild dogs, unused extras that no one remembers having ordered, are scavenging through Bott's studios.

The real Korda was indeed as eccentric as Dell's fictional parody suggests. As historian Sarah Street writes of him, "Korda's Hungarian background, flamboyant personality, craving for respectability, political connections, sensational financial deals, and alleged espionage activities have captured the imagination of both critics and supporters." Korda was a director as well as a producer. He gave the British film industry its first major international success with **The Private Life of Henry VIII** (1933), a deliberately saucy and over-the-top biopic of the Tudor monarch that won its bellowing star Charles Laughton a Best Actor Oscar. Its enormous box-office success provided Korda with respectability and, more importantly, business leverage. The Prudential Assurance Company, which normally gave film producers a very wide berth, began to support him the following year, pumping a reported $9.5 million into his endeavors. With Prudential backing, he not only transformed his company London Films (with its famous logo of Big Ben) into the UK's pre-eminent production outfit. He also secured a seat on the Board of United Artists and built himself his own new studio at Denham, north-west of London.

There was veiled anti-Semitism in the disapproval of Korda, this eastern European émigré seen by many as a crook when his business interests began to post huge losses. Nonetheless, his contribution to British film culture of the 1930s and 1940s can't be understated. In an industry that was parochial and inward looking, he was a cosmopolitan with a true international perspective—he had worked in continental Europe and Hollywood before he landed up in England. Korda was able to gather around him a group of extraordinarily talented fellow émigrés, among them many other Hungarians.

Britain didn't have its equivalent to the western, but Korda and his brothers Vincent and Zoltan made up for it with rip-roaring imperial adventures like **The Four Feathers** (1939) and **The Drum** (1938). Korda delved into sci-fi with H.G. Wells' adaptation **Things to Come** (1936) and into the realm of extravagant fantasy with **The Thief of**

01 Alexander Korda and Cary Grant (c.1947)

02 Alexander Korda with Merle Oberon, Laurence Olivier, Robert Taylor, and Tim Whelan (1937)

> "I think of him with affection—even love—as the only film producer I have ever known with whom I could spend days and nights of conversation without so much as mentioning the cinema."

Bagdad (1940). The latter film's co-director Michael Powell testified to his immense charm. "He [Korda] was tall, ugly, and elegant, spoke all European languages with a Hungarian accent, smoked nothing but large Coronas, and ate at all the best restaurants, lived at the Savoy. He was sociable, cultivated, and generous...everyone wanted to know Korda and Korda knew everyone."

As Powell's remarks attest, Korda conformed to what people expected of movie producers. He combined charm with raffishness and he projected an air of glamor and mystery. During World War II, he threw himself into the war effort, making propaganda films, lobbying the Americans to come into the war and earning himself a knighthood in the process. Korda may have been an erratic businessman and an infuriating collaborator, but the talent trusted him. He was a star-maker, identifying the screen potential of such actors as Laughton, Robert Donat, and Merle Oberon, and helping Laurence Olivier make the transition from stage to screen in films like **Lady Hamilton** (1941) and **Fire Over England** (1937). Korda was also able to compete on equal terms with ruthless Hollywood operators like David O. Selznick—with whom he tussled for credit and box-office revenue on Carol Reed's classic thriller **The Third Man** (1949). He also had the sometimes-grudging respect of novelist Graham Greene, whom he spurred into writing the screenplay for **The Third Man**.

Greene's remarks about Korda speak to why he was so popular with so many collaborators—namely that he didn't bear grudges and could see beyond the backbiting British movie business. "There was never a man who bore less malice," Greene wrote in his memoir *Ways of Escape*. "I think of him with affection—even love—as the only film producer I have ever known with whom I could spend days and nights of conversation without so much as mentioning the cinema."

03 That Hamilton Woman/Lady Hamilton (1941) starring Laurence Olivier and Vivien Leigh

04 Things To Come (1936), star Raymond Massey and directed by William Cameron Menzies

05 Charles Laughton in The Private Life of Henry VIII (1933)

Glossary

Assistant director (AD) The director's right-hand person, also called the first assistant director. Depending on the scope of the film, there can be second ADs and additional seconds.

Associate producer One of the lowest producer credits available, though often directly disproportionate to the amount of work the bearer of this credit has done on a film.

Auteur A filmmaker—usually a writer-director—with a strong personal vision who leaves a distinctive mark on a film, regardless of the many other collaborators involved.

Below-the-line Refers to the technical crews and costs related mainly to the physical production and post-production of a film. Salaries of starring actors, directors, writers and producers are considered "above-the-line" items.

CGI Computer-generated imagery, used to create fully digitally animated films or special effects work in live-action films.

Close-up A shot that focuses on an actor's face or is close enough to an object that not much of the background or surrounding imagery can be seen.

Completion bond An insurance contract to guarantee the producer will finish and deliver a film as per the agreed script, budget, and schedule. If a film is delayed or can't be completed, the bond covers the costs for investors.

Coproducer A producer credit that connotes a slightly less elevated position than a full "producer" credit. While not linked to a specific type of role in the making of a film, on international coproductions the credit can go to a producer whose company is not the lead production entity.

Coproduction A film involving multiple production partners and financing, usually from more than one country.

Creative producer A producer who is intensively involved in seeking out material, developing the script and putting together the creative filmmaking team.

Dailies The footage from the previous day's shooting, which allows the filmmakers to gauge performances and other aspects while the film is being shot.

Deferment A delayed compensation for cast or crew that isn't paid out until there are sufficient profits from the exploitation of the film to cover it.

Development The period before a project is ready to shoot during which the script is fleshed-out and refined, cast and crew decisions are weighed, and financing plans are put together.

Digital A moviemaking technology that, like traditional film, captures an image. Unlike celluloid, though, digital offers a more uniform image that lacks grain or the randomness of color and light.

Digital intermediate (DI) A technology that allows filmmakers the ability to tweak a film's color and image in post-production. DIs also can help filmmakers blow up 16mm to 35mm with more fidelity than was previously possible.

Distributor The company that acquires licensing rights to a film for exploitation in cinemas and on other distribution platforms, such as DVD, cable/satellite, and television.

DoP (director of photography)/cinematographer The head of the camera department, primarily responsible for all the photographic elements of a film.

Executive producer A nebulous credit that generally goes to a financier or the person who raised the financing for a film. It can also be given to individuals who are related to a film in other ways, such as talent managers who represent important actors, directors or writers on the film.

First-look deal A deal or option through which a studio has first right of refusal to a project that was developed under a producer deal at the studio.

Foreign sales company A company/agent that acquires and/or represents the overseas rights to motion pictures and then licenses these rights to individual distributors in countries/territories around the world. Also called "international sales."

Foreign sales estimates Dollar figures ascribed to the potential value of the international rights to a film project in the works. Estimates are usually based on the film's cast, director, and genre.

French New Wave A film movement that began in the late 1950s, emphasizing experimentation with the conventional Hollywood storytelling style. Led by directors such as Jean-Luc Godard and Francois Truffaut, French filmmakers adopted untraditional editing techniques (such as jump cuts) and handheld cameras for a more liberated and adventurous spirit. **Breathless** and **The 400 Blows** are considered landmarks of the movement.

Greenlight The go-ahead given by a studio or financier for a film to be made. When a film is greenlit it moves from the development stage to pre-production and on to principal photography, or production.

Greenscreen A special effects technique whereby actors or models are originally shot against a green or blue screen and then seamlessly imposed on a digitally rendered background that gives the appearance of another environment.

Independent/indie film A film made outside of the traditional Hollywood studio system, usually with money from private investors at a lower budget. In recent years, the indie film definition has broadened to bigger-budget films, often financed through foreign presales, that can end up being released by studios.

Line producer The person reporting to the main producer or studio, who oversees the day-to-day operations of a production and keeps the budget in check.

Location shooting Filming that is done in existing locations, rather than on sound stages and sets.

Mailroom The mail distribution hub of an agency or studio—traditionally the first point of entry into Hollywood for any aspiring talent agents and film executives.

Material The story and/or concept basis for a film project. This could include a book, a magazine or newspaper article, a script, a comic book, a play, a TV show, or someone's life story.

Mise-en-scène The "putting in place" or the way a scene film is framed, designed, and shot.

Negative pick-up A deal in which a studio or other distribution entity agrees to acquire the rights to a yet-to-be-completed film. It's a popular route for filmmakers who are able to find independent financing to make their films, as it generally keeps the creative control with the filmmakers.

Physical production The work done mainly during principal photography, when a film is being shot.

Points Percentage of a film's revenues (with "gross" or "net" making a huge difference) through which a producer can receive payment. If a film does well, it's usually the only way for a producer to earn any real money.

Post-production The period between the end of shooting and the release of the film. This is when the editing, special effects, scoring and dubbing are done.

Pre-production The stage immediately following a film being greenlit and the run-up to principal photography. Ideally during this time a film's script, cast, crew, and financing are finalized.

Pre-sale A deal struck for distribution rights before a film is completed, usually on the basis of the cast, script or filmmakers.

Principal photography The time during which a project is being shot and considered to be "in production," typically spanning a number of weeks. It is followed by post-production.

Producer deal Traditionally, a multi-year agreement for a producer to develop and produce films at a particular studio, usually accompanied by overhead money and a first-look option. These deals have become increasingly rare.

Producer fee A producer's main salary, usually paid upon completion of a film by a studio or other financier. At times, a producer may receive an advance on the fee, often at the time when their project is optioned by a studio.

Production assistant (PA) An entry-level, sometimes unpaid, job on a film production, with duties that involve running minor though tedious errands. Often a stepping stone to a moviemaking career.

Public funding Financing for film production provided by a government body or subsidy rather than through the private sector.

Reader A person who reads and gives comments—also known as "coverage"—on a script, usually working on a freelance basis or in an entry-level position for a studio, production company or talent agency.

Recoupment corridor A mechanism through which investors in film projects are repaid by revenues made from the film. It is often a matter of fierce negotiation as to who receives the monies in the first instance.

Rehearsal The process before the camera rolls where the actors practice how a scene will play out. Rehearsals can happen during pre-production as well as on set.

Rough cut A rough draft, if you will, of a film that allows the filmmakers to get a sense of the movie's overall flow before doing more tightening and trimming in the editing process.

Sales agent A person who negotiates and sells the distribution rights to a film.

Soft money Financing for film production available in the form of tax credits, rebates, and incentives that are offered by states and countries to encourage local investment. For example, if a producer shoots in Malta, thereby bringing money and employment to the island, that producer can claim a substantial rebate on local expenditures.

Storyboard A drawing that gives a blueprint for how an image (or a series of images) should look through the camera's viewfinder. Filmmakers will use storyboards to help illustrate their ideas before setting up a shot.

Story department The office, mainly at studios and other production companies, that oversees script coverage and keeps track of scripts, books and other material submitted for potential film projects. It is run by the story editor.

Index

8½ Women 90, *90*
13 Assassins 172
21 Grams 61, *68*
28 Days Later 127, *135*, 136
28 Weeks Later 134, 136

Alfredson, Tomas 24, 30
Aliens 3 117, 121
Amateur Night at the Dixie Bar and Grill 155
Amazing Grace 139
American Psycho 147, *147*
American Splendor 69
Anna Karenina (2012) 23
Antichrist 20
Any Given Sunday 153, 161
Armstrong, Gillian 33, 34–5, 36
Artist, The 8
Atonement 23, 24, 28, *31*
Au revoir les enfants 73, 79, 80
Australian New Wave 33, 35
Avatar 9, 117, 118, 122, *122*, 123, *123*

Babel 95, 100, *100*
Bad Lieutenant 139, 148, *148*
Bad Lieutenant: Port of Call-New Orleans 144, *149*
Bad and The Beautiful, The 11
Bad Timing 163, 165, *165*, 167, 171
Badlands 142, 145, *145*
Balcon, Michael 9, 46–7, *46*, 163
Bangalore Bullet 149
Barrett, Shirley 33, *36*
Basquiat 95, *99*, 102
Beach, The 127, 132, *132*, 134–5, 136
Bean movies 9, 23, *29*
Beat Street 119
Beat, The 95, 97–8
Beatty, Warren 117, 121, 125, 143, 153
Beautiful Country, The 139
Beauty and the Beast 86
Before Night Falls 99, 103
Berger, Albert 174–85, *174*, *176*, *182*, *185*
Bertolucci, Bernardo 163, 171, 173, *173*

Bevan, Tim 9, 10, 22–31, *22*, *25*, 166
Bier, Susanne 13, 14, 15, *15*, 16, 17, 20
Big Lebowski, The 23
Billy Elliot 23
Blood Simple 10, 97
Blood Sisters 142, *142*
Blue Kite, The 105, 106–7, 111
Blue Steel 139
Bob Roberts 102
Box, Betty 164
Boyle, Danny 9, 10, 127, *129*
Breaking the Waves 9, 17, *17*, 19–20
Bridget Jones's Diary movies 9, 23, 26, *26*, 31
Bright Star 33, 40, 42, *42*, 44
Broadcast News 143
Bronx Tale, A 95, 102, *103*
Brother Can You Spare A Dime 165
Brothers McMullen, The 61, 64, 66
Bruckheimer, Jerry 8, 147
Bulworth 153
Burns, Ed 61, 64, *64*, 66

Cameron, James 9, 10, 117, 118, 120, *120*, 121, *122*, 123
Campion, Jane 33, 34, 35–43, *39*, *42*
Campus Man 117, 118, *118*, 119
Certified Copy 81
Chabrol, Claude 9, 73, 77, *77*, 78, 80
Chaplin, Charles 78, *78*
Chapman, Jan 32–45, *32*, *37*, *39*, *42*
Chariots of Fire 9
Christie Malry's Own Double-Entry 85
Cleo From 5 to 7 74, 80, *80*
Close-Up 78
Coen brothers 10, 23, 25, 62, 64, 95, 97, 127, 128
Cold Mountain 175, *182*, 183
Conan the Barbarian 115, 139, 141, *141*, 143, 145–6
Cook, The Thief, His Wife and Her Lover, The 87, 89,

89, 91–2
Cooler, The 144
Cotton Club, The 119
Coup pour coup 74
Cradle Will Rock 102
Crash 0
Crouching Tiger, Hidden Dragon 9, 105, 107, 108, 109, *109*, 110
Crow, The 144, 148
Crusade in Jeans 85
Curse of the Golden Flower 111

Dancer in the Dark 19
Dangerous Mind, A 167
Dark Horse 61, *71*
Dave 153, *159*
De Beauregard, Georges 9
De Laurentiis, Dino 10, 114–15, *114*
De Niro, Robert 95, 98, 102, *103*
Dead Man Walking 102, *102*
Dear Phone 87
Devil Inside, The 56, *58*
Devil's Advocate, The 56
Di Bonaventura, Lorenzo 48–59, *48*, *52*, *57*
Dick Tracey 117, 121, 125, *125*
Dirty Dancing 98
Diving Bell and the Butterfly, The 95, *99*, 103
DNA 127, 133, 136, 137
Do the Right Thing 95, *96*, 98, 102
Doctor Reitzer's Fragment 128
Dogme 13, 16, 18
Dogville 20
Donner, Lauren Shuler 9, 152–61, *152*, *157*, *159*, *160*, *161*
Draughtsman's Contract, The 87, *87*
Drowning by Numbers 86, 90

Ealing Studios 9, 46–7
Edko 10, 105, 106, 112
Election 175, 176, 178–9, *178*, *179*
Element of Crime, The 14, *14*

Endurance 139
Enfer, L' 77
Epidemic 13, 14
Eureka 171
Europa 9, 13, 15–16, *16*
Every Man for Himself 73, 80

Falling Down 56
Falls, The 87
Fargo 23, *25*
Fellner, Eric 9, 11, 23, 24, 25, *25*, 29, 31, 166
Fish Tank 85, 92, 93, *93*
Flirt 70
Flowers of War, The 111, 113, *113*
Focus Features 61, 69
Food for Love 85
Found Money 119
Four Brothers 57, *57*, 58
Four Weddings and a Funeral 23, 27, *27*, 30, 136
Free Willy 153, *159*, 161
French New Wave 77, 80, 142

Garner, Helen 33, 34, 36
G.I. Joe movies 49, 51, *51*, 52, 58
Godard, Jean-Luc 9, 10, 73, 74, 75, 77–8, 80
Golan, Menahem 10
Goltzius and the Pelican Company 85, 88
Gone With the Wind 82, *82*, 83, *83*
González Iñárritu, Alejandro 61, 95, 100, *100*
Good Machine 61, 64, 67, 69, 70, 109
Good Morning, Babylon 146, *146*
Great Rock 'n' Roll Swindle, The 171
Green Zone 30–1, *30*
Greenaway, Peter 43, 85, 86–92, *89*
Griff the Invisible 33, *45*
Grillo, Janet 62, 64

H is for House 87
Haggis, Paul 9
haine, La 10
Hand, The 139

Happiness 61
Happy Times 139
Harris, Ed 95, *98*, 102
Hartley, Hal 61, 63
Haynes, Todd 10, 61, 64, *65*
Hazanavicius, Michel 8
Hero 105, 110, *110*
History Boys, The 127, 133, 136
Holy Smoke 40, 41, *41*
Honey, I Shrunk the Kids 117, 119, *119*, 125
Hope, Ted 60–71, *60*, *64*, *66*, *69*, *70*
Hotel for Dogs 153, 161
House of Flying Daggers 108
Hunger Games, The 95, 101, *101*
Hurt Locker, The 117

Ice Storm, The 61, 66, *66*, 67–8
Idiots, The 18, *18*
In the Bedroom 61, 67, *67*
In a Better World 17

Jarmusch, Jim 10, 62, 64, 95, 97
Jensen, Peter Aalbaek 9, 10, 12–21, *12*, *15*
Jungle Fever 95, 102

Karmitz, Martin 72–81, *72*, *75*, *77*, *81*
Kasander, Kees 84–93, *84*
Kassovitz, Mathieu 10
Ken Park 85, 91, *91*
Kiarostami, Abbas 73, 78, 79, 80, 81, *81*
Kieslowski, Krzysztof 73, 76, *76*
Kilik, Jon 94–103, *94*, *100*
King of the Hill 175, 176, *177*
Kingdom, The 17
Kong, Bill 9, 10, 104–13, *104*
Korda, Alexander 186–7, *186*
Kuhn, Michael 23, 25, 28

Ladyhawke 153, 158
Landau, Jon 9, 10, 116–25, *116*, *123*
Lantana 32, 33, *40*, 44
Last Days of Chez Nous, The

33, 34, 36
Last Emperor, The 8, 9, 163, 168, *168–9*, 171–2, 173
Last King of Scotland, The 127, 133, 136
Last of the Mohicans, The 117, 121, 124, *124*
Lawrence of Arabia 11
Lawrence, Ray 32, 33, 44
Lean, David 11
Lee, Ang 60, 61, 65, 66, 105, *107*, 108, 109, 111, 112, *112*
Lee, Spike 10, 62, 64, 95, 97, 98, 102, 128
Les Miserables 23
Life Less Ordinary, A 127, 131, 135, 137
Little Buddha 172, 173
Little Children 116, 183
Little Miss Sunshine 175, 181, *181*, 185
Lolita 108
Louder Than Bombs 175
Love Actually 23
Love Serenade 33, *36*
Lust, Caution 105, 111, 112, *112*

Macdonald, Andrew 8, 9, 10, 11, 126–37, *126*, *129*
Mad Dog Morgan 166, *166*
Madame Bovary 73, 77
Makhmalbaf, Mohsen 78, 79
Malcolm X 95, 97
Malle, Louis 73, 77, 80
Mann, Michael 121, *124*
Martha Marcy May Marlene 70, 71
Matrix, The movies 49, 54, *54–5*, 55–6
Meistrich, Larry 63–4
Melancholia 20–1, *21*
Mélo 73, 75, *75*
Merry Christmas Mr. Lawrence 170, *170*, 171
Minnelli, Vincente 11
Miral 103
Miramax 10, 33, 67, 144, 182
Mo' Better Blues 95, 97
Moth Diaries, The 147, 148
Mr. Mom 153, 155, *155*, 158

Mutant Chronicles 148
My Beautiful Laundrette 23, 25, *25*, 27

Naked Lunch 167
Nanny McPhee movies 23, 26, *26*, 31
Nebraska 175
Necessary Death of Charlie Countryman, The 175
Never Let Me Go 136, *136*, 137
Nightwatching 88, 90, *90*
Notes on a Scandal 127, 133, 136, *137*
Notting Hill 23, 29, *29*, 136
Noyce, Phillip 33, 34, 35

Ocean Heaven 105, 111
On Top of the Whale 85, 86
Oshima, Nagisa 170, *170*, 171
Out of It 140, *142*
Over Your Cities Grass Will Grow 85, *92*

Parole Officer, The 137
Passport To Pimlico 46, 163
Perfect Storm, The 56, *58*
Perfect World 10, 13, 14
Pervert's Guide to Cinema, The 85
Phantom of the Paradise 144–5
Piano, The 32, 33, 36, 37–40, *38*, *39*, 44
Picnic at Hanging Rock 35, *35*
Pillow Book, The 90
Pirates of Penzance, The 146, 147
Pleasantville 95, 101, 102
Plenty 146
Poison 65
Pollock 95, *98*, 102
Pommer, Erich 150–1
Pressburger, Emeric 10, 127
Pressman, Ed 138–49, *138*, *140*, *146*, *147*
Pretty in Pink 153, 158, *158*
Pride and Prejudice 28, *28*, 31
Prospero's Books 88, *88*, 90

Pulp Fiction 69, 70
Pushing Hands 61, 65, 107, 108
Puttnam, David 9, 24, 130, 165, 166

Rabbit Proof Fence 172
Radclyffe, Sarah 23, 25
Red 49, 59, *59*
Resnais, Alain 73, 75, *75*, 77, 78
Reversal of Fortune 139
Revolutionary, The 140
Roeg, Nicolas 163, 165, *165*
Ross, Gary 95, 102
Royal Affair, A 13
Ruby Sparks 175, 176, *184*, 185
Ruiz, Raoul 85, 86
Run Lola Run 10
Rush 23

Safe 10, 61
St. Elmo's Fire 153, 158, *158*
Salt 49, *55*
Savages, The 61, 65
Schamus, James 61, 63, *66*
Schnabel, Julian 95, 102
School Daze 98
Secret Life of Bees, The 153, 161, *161*
Selznick, David O. 8, 24, 82–3, *82*, 181
Sense and Sensibility 66
Sex, Lies, and Videotape 10, 129, 176
Shallow Grave 8, 127, 128–30, *128-9*, 131, 136
Shaun of the Dead 23, *25*
Sheltering Sky, The 9, 171, 172, 173
She's Gotta Have It 10, 97, 129
She's the Man 161
She's the One 64, *64–5*, 66
Shout, The 166, *166*, 170, 171
Silence, The 37
Skins 102
Snider, Stacy 28
Soderbergh, Steven 10, 56, 117, 175, 176, 177
Solaris 117, *125*
Somersault 33, *43*

Spiegel, Sam 8, 11
Springtime in a Small Town 105, *106*
Star Chamber, The 155
Stone, Oliver 10, 95, 139, 141, 143, 146, 153
Suburban Mayhem 33, *44*
Sunshine 133, *133*, 137
Switch, The 177–8, *180*, 182

Talk Radio 139, 146
Tall Guy, The 29
Taste of Cherry 78, 79
Thalberg, Irving 8
Thank God It's Friday 155
Thank You for Smoking 144
Thomas, Jeremy 8, 9, 10, 162–73, *162*, *164*, *165*, 173
Three Colors trilogy 73, 76, *76*, 78
Three Fugitives 161
Three Kings 56, *56*
Tian Zhuangzhuang 105
Tideland 172
Tinker Tailor Soldier Spy 24, 30, *30*, 31
Titanic 9, 107, 117, 118, 120, *120*, 121–2, *121*, 125, 127
Training Day 56, 58
Trainspotting 8, 10, 127, 130–1, *130–1*, 133, 135
Transformers movies 49, *50*, 52, 53, *53*, 54, 55, 58
True Lies 117, 121
True Stories 139
Trust 63, 65
Two Friends 33, 34, 36, 40
Tykwer, Tom 10

Unbelievable Truth, The 61, *62*, 63
Under the Hawthorn Tree 112
Undertow 139
United 93 30–1

Vachon, Christine 10, 64
Varda, Agnes 9, 74, 80
Von Trier, Lars 9, 13, 14–21, *15*

Walk the Talk 33
Walking and Talking 61, 63

Wall Street 139, 143, *143*, 148
Wall Street: Money Never Sleeps 139, 143, *143*, 147–8
Wedding Banquet, The 61, 64, *64*, 65, 68
Weinstein, Bob 10–11
Weinstein, Harvey 11, 63, 67, 69
Wind Will Carry Us, The 73, 79, *79*
Wolverine, The 153
Woman, a Gun and a Noodle Shop, A 101
Working Title Films 9, 11, 23, 25–31

X-Men movies 9, 153, 156, *156*, 161

Yerxa, Ron 174–85, *174*, *176*, *182*, *185*
You've Got Mail 9, 153, 160, *160*, 161

Zed & Two Noughts, A 87, 90
Zentropa 13, 15, 16, 17, 20
Zhang Yimou 105, *107*, 111, 113, *113*, 139

Picture Credits

Courtesy of the AFI/Photograph by Serge Thomann: 37T.

Alamy/Moviestore Collection Ltd: 131T; Photos 12: 91.

Courtesy of Albert Berger & Ron Yerxa: 176, 182B, 185B.

Courtesy of Lorenzo di Bonaventura: 52B, 52C.

Courtesy of Jan Chapman: 40B; Courtesy of Jan Chapman Films: 32T, 41BL; Courtesy of Jan Chapman Productions: 36T, 39T.

Corbis/Andrew Macpherson/Corbis Outline: 22T; Jeff Zelevansky: 64T.

Getty Images/Robin Beck/AFP: 48T; Richard Blanshard: 164; Eric Charbonneau/WireImage for Fox Searchlight Pictures: 174 T; Jamie McCarthy for Vanity Fair: 42CL; Kiyoshi Ota: 84T; Alberto E. Rodriguez: 162T; Chris Weeks/FilmMagic: 69B; Kevin Winter: 25TR.

Courtesy of Ted Hope: 60, 64B, 66B, 70.

Courtesy of Marin Karmitz/MK2: 75R, 76L, 77T, 81TR; Photograph by Benoît Linero: 72T.

Courtesy of Jon Kilik/Photograph used by permission of Jon Kilik: 100CL.

The Kobal Collection: 46L, 78, 82R; 150, 186L; 20th Century Fox: 65BL, 65BR, 132, 143TL, 155; 20th Century Fox/Frank Connor: 124TL; 20th Century Fox/Fox Searchlight Pictures: 181T; 20th Century Fox/Fox Searchlight Pictures/David Lee: 174B; 20th Century Fox/Fox Searchlight Pictures/Eric Lee: 181B; 20th Century Fox/Bob Marshak: 125B; 20th Century Fox/Morgan Creek/Frank Connor: 124B, 20th Century Fox/Paramount: 120CR; 20th Century Fox/Paramount/Digital Domain: 120T; A2/MK2: 75L; AAFC/Doll/New South Wales Film & TV: 44; AAFC/Showtime Australia: 43; AIP: 142T; Allarts: 86; Allarts/Camera 1/Cinea: 88, 90TL; Allarts/Erato: 89; Allarts/Vpro/BFI/Channel Four: 2, 90R; Anonymous Content/Dune Films: 94B, 100B, 100T; Arte France/Blind Spot/Dinovi: 19; BBC Films: 32B, 42TR, 42B, 42CR, 93; Beijing Film Studio: 106; Beijing New Picture Film Co.: 107B; Beijing New Picture Film Co./Edko Film: 113; Beijing New Picture Film Co./Elite Group: 110, 104B; Beijing New Picture Film Co./IDG/New Classical Entertainment: 112TR; Beijing New Picture Film Co./Sony pictures Classics/Bai Xiao Yan: 111; Beyond Films/Jan Chapman Productions: 40T; BFI/United Artists: 87; Big Talk/WT 2/Oliver Upton: 25BR; Bona Fide Productions: 180, 184, 185T; Brant-Allen/Demmie Todd: 98; Peter Brooker: 104T; CAB/FR3/Canal+: 76B Canal+: 81TL, 81B; Central Motion Pictures/Good Machine: 64T; Channel 4 Films/Glasgow Film Fund: 128, 129BL; Channel 4/Kanzaman/Nick Wall: 6, 162B; China Film Group Corporation/Bai Xiao Yan: 108; Ciby 200/Recorderd Picture Co.: 173BL; Columbia Pictures: 55T, 158L; Columbia/Sony: 107T; Columbia/Sony/Chan Kam Chuen: 109; ContentFilm/Dog Pond/Lions Gate: 144T; ContentFilm International: 90BL; De Laurentiis: 141; De Laurentiis/20th Century Fox, Louis Goldman: 115R; Decla/Bioscop: 151L DNA Films: 136L, 136BR; DNA/Figment/Fox/Peter Mountain: 135; Double Hope Film: 71T; Dreamworks: 53C; Dreamworks/Robert Zuckerman: 53B; Ealing: 47L; Ealing/Rank: 46R; Edward R. Pressman Film: 143BL, 148; Electric Pictures: 62; Eleventh Street Productions/Miramax: 99R; Elmar Pictures/Daniel Daza: 99TL; Figment/Noel Gay/Channel 4: 126B, 130, 131BL; Film Fyn: 17R; Filmtre/Mk2/Pressman/Rai/Films A2: 146TR; Focus Features/Alex Bailey: 31; Focus Features/Chan Kam Chuen: 112BR, 112L; Focus Features/Merrick Morton: 68TL, 68TR; Focus Features/Jim Sheldon: 68B; Focus Features/Greg Williams: 22B; Fox Atomic/DNA Films/UK Film Council/Susie Allnut: 134; Fox Searchlight Pictures: 60, 71B, 133B, 144B, 161R; Fox Searchlight/Alex Bailey: 133T; Fox Searchlight/Clive Coote: 137BR; Fox Searchlight/Neil Davidson: 137BR; Good Machine: 66T; Good Machine/Barry Wetcher: 66C; Good Machine/Greenestreet/Standard Film/John Clifford: 67; Good Machine/HBO/John Clifford: 69TR, TL; Gramercy Pictures: 177; Green Park Pictures: 45; Hachette Premiere/Kushner-Locke Co./Severine Brigeot: 173R; Insurg Pictures: 58T; ITV Global: 47R, 103, 165R, 166, 187R, 187TL, 187BL; Jan Chapman Productions/AFFC: 34; Jan Chapman Productions/Ciby 2000: 38, 39; Jan Chapman Productions/Elise Lockwood: 36B; JF Productions/Recorded Picture Company: 171; Kasander & Wigman/Alpha Films/Mark Guillamot: 84B; Lightstorm/20th Century Fox: 121; Lionsgate: 101; Lionsgate/Kerry Hayes: 147B; London-Denham Films/United Artists: 186R; Marvel/20th Century Fox: 152B, 156B; Marvel/20th Century Fox/Attila Dory: 156T; MGM: 83TL; Millennium Films: 149; Miramax: 182T; Miramax/Dimension Films/Penny Tweedie: 172L; Miramax/Gerald Jenkins: 41R, 47TL; Miramax/Universal/Alex Bailey: 26L; Miramax/Universal/Studio Canal/Laurie Sparham: 26BR MK2 Productions/CED Productions: 77BL; MK2/Abbas Kiarostami Productions: 79B; MK2/CED/CAB: 72B; MK2/CED/France 3: 77R; MK2/CED/France 3/TOR/Canal+: 76CR, 76T; New Line/Bona Fide Productions/Robert Zuckerman: 183; Nordisk/SFI/DFI/Eurimages: 12B, 16; Nouvelles Editions/Mk2/Stella/Nef: 79T; October Films: 65T; Paramount Pictures: 48B, 50, 51, 52T, 53T, 114, 115L, 118, 158R; Paramount Pictures/Bob Akester: 178, 179; Paramount Pictures/Di Bonaventura Pictures Production: 57T; Paramount Pictures/Di Bonaventura Pictures Production/George Kraychyk: 57B; Pathé: 99BL; Per Holst Film Prod: 14; Picnic/BEF/Australian Film Commission: 35; Polygram: 29TL, 137L; Polygram/Channel 4/Working Title: 27; Polygram/Clive Coote: 29TR; Polygram/Suzanne Hanover: 29B; Polygram/Propaganda/Juergen Teller: 37B; Pressman/Most: 138B; Rank: 165L; Recorded Pic-Cineventure-Asahi/Oshima: 170; Recorded Picture Company: 167B; Recorded Picture Company/First Independent: 167T; RPC: 172TR; SARA/MK2/SAGA: 80; Sciapode/Kasander Film/Amoeba Film: 92; Sedic/RPC/Dentsu: 172BR; Selznick/United Artists: 83BL; Selznick/MGM: 82L, 83R; Studio Canal: 30TL, TR; Summit Entertainment: 59; Touchstone: 125T; Twentieth Century-Fox Film Corporation: 5, 116B, 122, 123B; UFA: 151R, 151C; Universal Pictures: 26CR, 30B, 96, 97B; Universal/Working Title: 26TR; Walt Disney: 119; Warner Bros.: 54, 55B, 56, 145, 159TL, 159B, 173TL; Warner Bros/Claudette Barius: 58B; Warner Bros./Brian Hamill: 160; Warner Bros/David Lee: 97T; Woodline/Movie Masters/Jaap Buitendijk: 90CL; Working Title/Alex Bailey: 28; Working Title/Channel 4: 25L; Working Title/Havoc: 102; Working Title/Polygram/Michael Tackett: 25CR; Yanco/Tao/Recorded Picture Co: 168, 169; Zenith Productions: 63; Zentropa: 17L, 18, 20B, 21; Zentropa/Rolf Konow: 20T; Zentropa/Two Brothers: 15R.

Courtesy of Jon Landau: 116T, 120C, 120B, 120CL, 123T, 123C, 124TR.

Courtesy of Lantana Productions: 40B.

Courtesy of Andrew Macdonald: 126T, 129T, 131BR.

Courtesy of Paramount Pictures. All Rights Reserved. Transformers © 2007 DW Studios L.L.C and Paramount Pictures Corporation. All Rights Reserved: 52B; Transformers: Revenge of the Fallen © 2009 DW Studios L.L.C. and Paramount Pictures Corporation. All Rights Reserved: 52C.

Press Association Images/AP Photo/Kevork Djansezian: 100CR.

Courtesy of Edward R. Pressman: 138T, 140, 142B, 143R, 146L, 146BR, 147T.

Rex Features/20th Century Fox/Everett Collection: 136TR; Mark O'Sullivan: 129BR.

Courtesy of Lauren Shuler Donner: 156C, 157BL, 157R 157TL, 159TR, 161L; Photograph by Greg Gorman: 152T.

Courtesy of TrustNordisk/Zentropa Productions: 12T, 15L.

Courtesy of Twentieth Century Fox. All rights reserved: Avatar © 2009 Twentieth Century Fox. All rights reserved: 123T, 123C; The Ice Storm © 1997 Twentieth Century Fox. All rights reserved/Good Machine: 66B; The Last of the Mohicans © 1992 Twentieth Century Fox. All rights reserved/Morgan Creek: 124TR; Ruby Sparks © 2012 Twentieth Century Fox. All rights reserved: 185B; The Secret Life of Bees © 2008 Twentieth Century Fox. All rights reserved: 161L; She's the One © 1996 Twentieth Century Fox. All rights reserved: 64B; Titanic © 1997 Twentieth Century Fox and Paramount Pictures Corporation. All rights reserved: 120C, 120B, 120CL; X-Men © 2000 Twentieth Century Fox. All rights reserved: 156C; X-Men: The Last Stand © 2006 Twentieth Century Fox. All rights reserved: 157TL; X2 © 2003 Twentieth Century Fox. All rights reserved: 157BL, 157R.

All images appear © their respective copyright holders. Every effort has been made to acknowledge the pictures, however, the publisher apologizes if there are any unintentional omissions.

Special thanks to Darren Thomas, Cheryl Thomas and all at The Kobal Collection for their effort and support.